AND GOD WAS WATCHING

- A Biography of Billy Wayne -

JANET GIBSON AND BILLY WAYNE ARRINGTON

CrossBooks™
A Division of LifeWay
1663 Liberty Drive
Bloomington, IN 47403
www.crossbooks.com
Phone: 1-866-879-0502

Edited By Brenda Gibson
Additional Editing Greg Belknap
Proofing Cindy Martin

©2011 Janet Gibson and Billy Wayne Arrington. All rights reserved.

Photography Credits
Vickie L. Collea (Theatre Cast)
Derek Cress (LampLight Theatre & Billy Wayne 2011)
Felicia Rowland

No part of this book may be reproduced, stored in a retrieval system, or transmitted by any means without the written permission of the author.

First published by CrossBooks 04/06/2011

ISBN: 978-1-6150-7744-1 (sc)
ISBN: 978-1-6150-7745-8 (hc)

Library of Congress Control Number: 2011922584

Printed in the United States of America

This book is printed on acid-free paper.

Any people depicted in stock imagery provided by Thinkstock are models, and such images are being used for illustrative purposes only.

Certain stock imagery © Thinkstock.

Because of the dynamic nature of the Internet, any web addresses or links contained in this book may have changed since publication and may no longer be valid. The views expressed in this work are solely those of the author and do not necessarily reflect the views of the publisher, and the publisher hereby disclaims any responsibility for them.

Contents

Foreword vii
Thanks to ix

Chapter 1	God Won! 1
Chapter 2	Midst the Storm 9
Chapter 3	A Life to Bargain 15
Chapter 4	Mountain Movers 19
Chapter 5	Loving the Unlovable 25
Chapter 6	Becoming a "Somebody" 39
Chapter 7	Bullies and Compassion 47
Chapter 8	Pull the Trigger 57
Chapter 9	Seeds of Bitterness 61
Chapter 10	Creating Character 67
Chapter 11	College Bound 73
Chapter 12	You Win, God 97
Chapter 13	Long-Awaited Words 103
Chapter 14	A New Mama 105
Chapter 15	Dreamcoats and Repentant Thieves 113
Chapter 16	Gifts for Ministry 117
Chapter 17	Kingdom's Call 125
Chapter 18	Tell Them 133
Chapter 19	Opened Doors 139
Chapter 20	Oh Ye, of Little Faith 145
Chapter 21	Sacred Mountains 149
Chapter 22	Acts of God 153
Chapter 23	God Is Still Watching 163

Epilogue 169

Foreword

A personal note from Billy Wayne

The fact that you are reading this foreword is amazing to me. I never thought this book would ever be written. It has been several years in the making. I know that God's timing is perfect and that you are the person this book was written for.

I am grateful for Janet Gibson, who has believed in this ministry and me for years. I know that she had major obstacles to overcome. From the tireless gathering of information to the patient prodding of my memories, her efforts have now come to fruition.

The stillness of God and writer's block led us to make this a collaborative effort for both of us. I never intended to be a joint writer, but God had other things in mind. Obviously, He won.

In an attempt to write a book of inspiration, feelings can be hurt as lives are exposed for everyone to view. It is the purpose of this book to let those who read it know the awesome power of God's forgiveness and healing. Bitterness can destroy people's lives and keep generations in bondage for years. Thank God for being the bondage breaker.

The information in this book is as accurate as the accounts that were given from all that were interviewed and from personal experience. I am certain that some details were not fully revealed in order to protect some innocent parties. Regardless, the book is a biography of the life of an ordinary person who met an extraordinary Savior who changed his life and the lives of those around him forever, me.

It is my prayer that God changes your life through these pages and you know that good things are often born from difficulties. May you be inspired to overcome your past to live a life of hope and forgiveness.

Thanks to:

My mom and dad, who did the best they could at raising a family without knowing Jesus and becoming my heroes when they gave their lives to Him. Thanks for believing in me and being my biggest supporters. You are the best.

My siblings, who have been more than patient over the years. Thanks for putting up with my "in your face" boldness. I would have disowned me more than once if I were you.

My family. You know the good, the bad, and the ugly, and you still love me. Some of you even choose to work with me. You are a gracious people. I love you.

My staff for your encouragement. This journey has been long, and you are the reason I can do what I do. Let's lead more to Jesus.

My executive board. Your advice and wisdom have made this ministry what it is. Thanks for standing in the gap and helping to accomplish the vision.

My friends and ministry partners. Friendship is one of the greatest indications of unconditional love. Thanks for your continued love and support.

My son, Ridgemond Mosley. You have taught me more about God's love than you will ever know. You are a trophy in God's display case. I cannot wait to see what God has ahead of you. Don't give up on yourself. God is watching you.

- Chapter 1 -

God Won!

The drive to the church that evening gave Billy some time to reflect on the past few years and the times he had crossed paths with Shawn Bennett. It was 2001, and the sun was beginning to sink into the early June sky as Billy neared Eden, North Carolina. The three-hour drive from his hometown of Kingsport, Tennessee, had been a time to reflect. He was beginning to realize that he would have to spend the rest of his life with things as they had stood between Shawn and himself, wondering if there had been anything left undone or unsaid. Had he been too harsh with Shawn, as he had been so many times before? Billy wished he could have been able to say good-bye. They had shared good times as well as bad times. Now he would have to recall their last conversation and let it stand—frozen in time, as it was. There would be no more apologies or a time to reconcile, only regrets.

Billy searched his memory for anything that he might use to console himself. Shawn had seemed to be on the road to recovery. He had been drug free for over a year, yet Billy had found it hard to trust him. Shawn had betrayed his trust so many times. He wondered if he had shown Shawn true friendship. He had so many questions and perhaps just as many regrets where Shawn was concerned.

He thought of the first time he had met Shawn. Billy had been doing a concert and telling the audience about redemption and God's forgiveness, no matter how far away we get from Him or what we are guilty of doing.

No one pointed Shawn out to him during the concert. No one had to. Billy could see a look in Shawn's eyes that he had seen a hundred times before—the look of hunger to hear more about being forgiven. Experience and the Holy Spirit had taught Billy about what that look meant. It meant a person was dealing with something bigger than they could handle, which certainly turned out to be the case with Shawn.

After the concert, Billy knew he had to find Shawn in the crowd. He knew he had to befriend Shawn and try to help him. He didn't know him. They had never even met before. It bothered Billy to see someone being so tormented in their soul when he knew they could be set free by the grace of God. He never stopped to consider what a friendship with Shawn might cost him or even the possibility that talking with him that night would grow into a lifelong, volatile friendship, with the highest highs and the lowest lows. He just knew that there was pain in Shawn's eyes and understood it more as Shawn talked to him that night of his struggles and his family. Billy had not dreamed of what the next few years would bring.

Shawn was addicted to crack cocaine, and anyone who has ever had their life touched by a crack addict knows the pain this substance can cause. As long as that person is using, everyone in that individual's life is taken advantage of, complete with broken promises, lies, and betrayals. Billy had always prided himself with being able to help people. He had always been able to fix what was wrong, helping people to overcome their problems. He was confident that if he spent enough time teaching Shawn about God and pointing him in the right direction, Shawn would be able to overcome his addictions and become the father he should be to Seth and the husband he should be to Bobbi Jo. Billy knew all too well what substance abuse of any kind can do to a family. He had lived with it in his family, and he recognized the pain Shawn was inflicting.

Drugs had become an escape for Shawn, an escape from a reality that was spinning out of control daily. Shawn knew he was losing the battle, but there was no fight left in him. He really wanted to quit using drugs, but the clutches of crack cocaine had already pitted its ugly claws deep into his flesh, refusing to let loose. He had surrendered to the addiction and the lie that would hold him in bondage for the rest of his life.

Shawn had a big heart, and he could be the kindest, most gentle person. His drug addiction made him something completely opposite of what had attracted Bobbi Jo to him in the first place. Shawn and Bobbi Jo had met when she was fourteen years old, and they had been together ever since. She loved the man she knew him to be when he wasn't using drugs. Her life revolved around trying to get Shawn the help he needed.

Bobbi Jo had been a Christian for many years, and she prayed often for Shawn's healing.

Billy had gained Shawn's respect from the moment they first met. There was something about Billy that drew Shawn into a friendship with him. He saw how Billy prayed and how he seemed to have a direct line to God. Shawn didn't believe that was possible for someone like himself. He had spent most of his years being told that he wasn't quite as good as everyone else. He believed that lie, and because of it, he didn't much like himself, either. For someone like Shawn, God seemed untouchable, and now here was this preacher, Billy Wayne, telling him that God loved him and wanted to know him better.

Shawn couldn't tune out what Billy was saying that night and wondered if it could be true. Could God really want a friendship with someone who had made such a mess of his life? No one had ever presented God as a loving God like this before. For the first time, Shawn began to feel like there was actually a ray of hope shining down from heaven for him. He wanted to know more. Was this the truth? Did God really care for him?

Shawn could barely contain himself at the thought of being "redeemed" and forgiven for all the things he had done wrong. He had carried around guilt for many years. He felt as though he had failed Bobbi Jo and Seth, which only added to the lie that he wasn't good enough.

After hearing the message that night about God's forgiveness, Shawn began his own search for God. He wrestled with God for many months, and finally one night, after watching an Easter drama at Osborne Baptist Church in Eden, North Carolina, Shawn gave his life to God. He was all too glad to be rid of the burdens he had been carrying around. He wept uncontrollably for what seemed like an eternity as Billy witnessed him asking God for forgiveness. Shawn was eager to learn more about God, and Billy was up to the challenge of teaching him.

Old habits die hard, especially drug habits. Shawn had the best intentions in the world, but his past hunted him like a hungry lioness hunting food for her cubs. He loved God and loved the fact that God had forgiven him, but he couldn't seem to shake his crack addiction. Shawn never broke the ties with his old friends, who were users themselves. He thought he would be strong enough to be around them without being tempted. He was wrong. The vicious cycle continued for the next several years. Shawn would stay clean for months at a time, but then, from out of the blue, his urges became too strong to resist. He would use again, follow up with a promise to never do it again, and then break his promise, which in itself made him feel like a failure over and over again.

When he was using, he would stay away from Billy. Billy always questioned him and got in his face about his addiction. Shawn didn't want to hear Billy's questions while he was on a binge, but guilt would get the best of him, and he would ultimately come to Billy and apologize many times over for not being a stronger Christian. Billy always encouraged Shawn. Shawn would listen to Billy when no one else could get through to him. He wanted so badly to be stronger. He needed Billy's friendship. He needed Billy's encouragement in his life.

For a long time after their friendship began, Billy was patient with Shawn. He had been around drug addicts enough to know that they are as disappointed with themselves as anyone else is when they slip into old habits. Billy spent many nights praying with Shawn till the early morning hours. He would sit with him and talk to him about how the things he was doing were causing so much pain for those who loved him. Shawn was always very remorseful. Billy had done everything in his power to keep Shawn from using, short of chaining Shawn to himself. He cared for Shawn and would have done whatever it took to see him completely free from the stronghold of his drug addiction.

Once, Shawn had told Billy of a drug dealer that was threatening to hurt Bobbi Jo and Seth if he didn't pay him the money he owed right away. He had told Billy that the dealer was calling the house and making threats. Because Shawn had taken advantage of him many times, Billy was leery to help him but finally told Shawn that he would give him the money to pay the man off. Billy insisted, however, that he would personally drive Shawn there and make sure he actually delivered the money. Shawn agreed. Billy drove Shawn to Logtown, just outside of Eden, so Shawn wouldn't be in that vicinity alone and be tempted to use again. Logtown had a reputation of being a rough neighborhood. It was the first time Billy had ever been there, but it would not be his last.

He followed Shawn's directions to where Shawn was to pay off the man that had been threatening his family. Billy parked the car in front of an old rundown store, just below a house trailer that sat up on a hill. Shawn nervously got out of the car and walked up to the trailer. Billy was just as nervous sitting in his car, waiting on Shawn to return. He wondered how he had gotten this involved with Shawn and if being seen here could cost him in his ministry.

A few moments passed, and Shawn emerged from the trailer and made his way back to the car. Billy asked him if he had delivered the money and if the dealer said he would leave Bobbi Jo and Seth alone now. Shawn's reply was "yes," but his actions told Billy there had been more of a conversation than Shawn would admit. Anxious to get out of Logtown, Billy quickly drove away with Shawn beside him and felt a sense of relief, believing this would be the last time Shawn would have any dealings with such people. He didn't follow his instincts to probe Shawn for further information.

Later in the day, Billy received a phone call from Bobbi Jo. Her words made him feel as angry as he could ever remember feeling. She said, "You've been had!"

Billy was confused at first and told Bobbi Jo that she would have to explain herself. Bobbi Jo went on to explain that Shawn had used Billy and his money to buy more drugs. He hadn't paid anyone any money, and as far as she could tell, there had not been any threats in the first place.

Anger shot through Billy as he recalled the desperation that Shawn had led him to feel about the threats. Billy had been conned, and he didn't take it lightly. Shawn had lied to Billy before when drugs were involved, but this would be the last time. Billy felt humiliated and manipulated. He didn't like being played for a fool. His face burned with anger at the thought of Shawn's betrayal. Shawn had just severed the last bit of trust that Billy had in him. Bobbi Jo knew what Shawn was capable of doing and had warned Billy on occasion to be careful. She didn't want to see Billy get hurt.

Billy vowed to separate himself from Shawn. He loved Shawn, but Shawn had exhausted his trust. He had given Shawn the best he had and tried to be the best friend he could be, but Shawn had tossed all of that aside for drugs.

Bobbi Jo had reached the point of alienating herself also. She had given up when Billy still had hope. Now there was no one who had hope for Shawn. Both his friend and his wife had lost all faith in his ever making a complete change.

Years earlier, soon after Bobbi Jo found out she was carrying his child, she had kicked Shawn out of the house. Shawn always knew that even if Bobbi Jo was mad at him and wouldn't speak to him, Billy would. Now, no matter how hard Shawn tried to get back into both of their lives, he could not succeed. Billy encouraged Bobbi Jo to be strong and resist him when he called. He urged her to separate herself and Seth from him indefinitely. Shawn had spiraled completely out of control, and there was no deception that went too far for him. He was now living on the streets and had no one. He had always been able to page Billy, and Billy would return his phone calls no matter how far away Billy was. Shawn had always found comfort in talking with Billy when his life was bad. Now, Billy wouldn't return his phone calls, and Bobbi Jo refused to let him come home. He had to make a choice. With no one to care what happened to him, he would surely die in this state. He missed his wife and son and his friendship with Billy. Could he change? Could he bring his drug addiction completely under control? He wasn't sure, but he was determined to regain what he had lost. He somehow managed to hold down his job as a mechanic despite his drug use. His road to recovery would be difficult, but he had full determination to be reinstated as a husband and friend.

He approached Bobbi Jo with the news that he was now clean. She had heard that line so many times before. Something in her heart told her that he was serious this time, but her past experiences with him told her not to trust him. The sincerity in his voice and in his eyes was different. He had been cut off from his family, and he was obviously miserable. Bobbi Jo couldn't deny the love she still had for him. It was the hardest thing she had ever done to keep turning him away when he needed her to help him. Something was different this time. She knew Billy would tell her not to trust Shawn, but she had to go with her instincts. She agreed to give him another chance. Shawn promised not to let her down. He started going to church with Bobbi Jo and Seth and surrounding himself with people whom he had previously given reason not to trust him. He knew how badly he had betrayed everyone, and he was determined to make it up to them by not only proving that he was not using drugs anymore, but by going above and beyond the call of friendship, especially where Billy Wayne was involved.

Billy wasn't going to be lured back into Shawn's world. He had been there ... done that, and had resolved within himself never to trust Shawn again. Maybe that was why he was feeling so much guilt now. He had never really given Shawn his total friendship again after he had betrayed Billy by conning him into giving him money and using it to buy drugs.

With Shawn's newfound life without drugs, he felt as though he had a lot of lost time to make up for. He had a keen ear when he was around Billy and would pick up on little things he would overhear Billy saying he needed, such as changing the oil in his van. Billy noticed Shawn's efforts, and he saw that Shawn became almost servant like around him. Knowing that Shawn would do anything for him, and not wanting to take advantage of his good nature, Billy found himself being cautious about what he said when Shawn was around.

Their friendship was back, but it was never the same. A trust had been broken and, though still in the mending stage, had never been completely repaired. But when Shawn suddenly died from a heart attack at the age of thirty-three, it all came to a screeching halt. Billy would spend the rest of his life wondering where he had gone wrong and what he could have done differently. Questions would always surface when he thought of Shawn. Did he give him the best he could give him? Did he follow God's lead in all situations with Shawn? Was this what it meant to be in ministry and give all you have?

Billy had always wanted to help people. He had always desired a gentle spirit and an ability to extend himself to help others who were in need. Had he done this with Shawn? The ministry of Vision Productions, Inc. came full circle with Shawn. It was in this friendship that Billy had to pause and ask God for direction many times. With Shawn's death, the idea of being a failure came crashing in on Billy. Did he have what it took to minister to people now? Would he be hesitant to ever help another drug addict? These were questions he would have to find the answers to before he could go on in the ministry.

Billy was nearing Eden, deep in thought. He had made the trip a hundred times, but this time, he missed the exit to get to the church. He decided to take the next exit and make his way back to Eden through the outskirts of the town. As he began to maneuver through back roads, he suddenly found himself in unfamiliar territory. Confused and needing to get his bearings, he pulled off to the side of the road. Immediately, he recognized the old rundown store and the house trailer that sat on the hill in front of him. It was the place where he had taken Shawn to pay off his dealer. He couldn't believe that he was here in this place, on this day: the day of Shawn's funeral! Totally frustrated at missing his exit, Billy cried out to God for help. He could not believe that he could be in this place today, of all days. Billy asked God why He was allowing this to happen to him today.

It was as if God spoke directly to Billy's soul as he stared at the little trailer where Shawn had made the choice to betray their friendship. God's words were simply, "I won!" At once Billy found peace in knowing that Shawn would never be tempted by drugs again. Shawn's days on earth were finished. He was now walking in God's glory! Billy began to understand betrayal that day. He knew that he had been hurt by Shawn's betrayal. Again, God gave him understanding that day of how we, as humans, betray God and how God forgives. Billy experienced an epiphany that day that further enlightened him on God's divine nature.

Billy eventually arrived at the church. Bobbi Jo had asked him to sing at the funeral. As Billy sang, he felt a new sense of forgiveness. He had completely forgiven Shawn for all he had held against him. Billy's only regret was that Shawn wasn't there. God had been gracious in the events earlier in the evening and the astounding way He chose to reveal betrayal and forgiveness to Billy.

As Billy was ending his tribute to Shawn, he stepped closer to Bobbi Jo. They had shared so many struggles with Shawn. There seemed to be a silent understanding of the guilt that each of them felt from not being able to trust Shawn in the last few months. They both wished now that they would have. As Billy looked directly at Bobbi Jo, he left her with the same words that God had spoken to him earlier: *God won!*

Billy's pastor, Steve Griffith, stood beside him as Shawn's casket was carried outside and passed to the waiting hearse. Steve must have known just what Billy was feeling, as he put his hand on Billy's shoulder and said, "Don't feel guilty. When the rest of us had given up, you loved this man into heaven."

Guilt was exactly what Billy was feeling. He knew he had loved Shawn unconditionally and was having a difficult time coming to grips with all the ups and downs of their friendship. For the first time since the news of Shawn's death, Billy found comfort in Steve's words.

- *Chapter 2* -

Midst the Storm

Spring was being ushered in as nature unleashed a fury of dark clouds over the southwestern Appalachian Mountains of Virginia. The western winds blew, and the angry clouds produced a downpour like many folks said they had never seen. It was as though each drop was splashing to the earth in a collaborated celebration of the new season. The day was March 6, 1963. The winter had not been especially cold, but spring would be most welcome. Days on end lacked sunshine. Bethel Arrington watched the drops of rain from inside the shelter of her mother-in-law Maudie's house in Speers Ferry, Virginia. It was the safest place to be, considering the circumstances.

The rain beat mercilessly against the tin roof of the house while the low rumble of thunder kept thoughts of a sunny day at bay. It sounded like a continuous thundering round of applause, perhaps applauding the victory of spring conquering winter, perhaps applauding another event that would soon take precedence over the concerns the rains had brought.

Bethel stroked her hand down over her stomach. It felt tight. She was small in stature and nine months pregnant, which combined to make her look most uncomfortable. Looking at her profile in the mirror as she stroked her stomach, she knew it would not be long. She thought of Mary Belle, her own mother, who had given birth to twelve children, which eased her mind; she knew that if Mary Belle could suffer through twelve deliveries, she could surely make it through her second one.

She wondered if this would be the day. The pounding rains kept her from making a premature decision to go to the hospital. The streams outside were rising and her pains were intensifying. Mammaw Maudie had insisted that Bethel and two-year-old Donna Lynn stay with her until this new baby was born. Cecil, Bethel's husband, worked long hours and was gone most of the day, so Bethel also thought it was probably a good arrangement. Cecil's younger sister, Betty Jo, was still living at home. She and Bethel were close in age and could keep each other company.

Maudie and Bethel had formed a close bond. Their relationship was more like a mother and daughter than that of in-laws. Bethel had been sixteen and Cecil, nineteen, when they had married. Bethel still had much to learn about being a wife and mother, and Maudie was willing to teach her. They had a common ground. Both women loved Cecil, and they truly loved one another.

A sharp pain in Bethel's back jolted her from her thoughts and reminded her that this baby may come sooner rather than later. Bethel was growing anxious with each passing moment. *If only Cecil were home now, he could get me to the hospital,* she thought. She was beginning to get frightened. The water outside would soon block them in with no easy access to the highway that led to the hospital.

Just then Cecil and his brother, Elmer, came through the door, shaking off the cold rain, relieved to find a dry refuge. Because of swollen streams, they had to walk the last half mile to the house. Cecil had left his car parked at a local store just down the road. They were working at Grief Brothers at this time, which was located about forty minutes away. Earlier in Cecil and Bethel's marriage, he boarded away from home most of the time. Bethel didn't like being alone while he was gone, and she urged him to find work closer to home, which he eventually did. Being born to a hard-working father who worked in the mines and a mother who wasn't afraid to work in the fields as well as keep house and tend to nine children, Cecil thought it completely normal to dedicate his life to making a living for his family, even at the expense of having to live away from them at times. He wanted a better way of life for his kids than what he had known.

His life as a child had been difficult. He and his brothers grew up with little material wealth, but they always had each other. His parents were good Christian people who instilled the truths about the grace of God in all their children. Cecil's father, Enoch, not only worked hard in the mines, but he also served the community as an undertaker of sorts. He would prepare corpses for viewing by shaving the men's faces and dressing them appropriately for burial. He would also plot out the actual grave sites and then oversee the digging of the graves. Cecil often helped with this unpopular yet necessary task.

On June 2, 1957, a pivotal point came in young Cecil's life. It was his sixteenth birthday. He and his dad, along with several other men in the community, were digging a grave. Cecil left the gravesite to get water for everyone. When he returned, he found Enoch lying on a blanket beside the grave they were digging. Water was running out of his mouth, and his skin was a pasty color. The men told Cecil that he had collapsed, and they laid him on the blanket so he could rest. Cecil was upset that the men had not taken his father to get help.

Believing that his dad needed immediate medical attention, Cecil sought the help of Bigfoot, a man who lived close by, to take them to the hospital. Most of the people in the community were afraid of Bigfoot. He had the reputation of being a drunk, but he helped Cecil that day when no one else would.

Enoch didn't survive the episode, and Cecil's heart became hardened toward the Christian men who didn't help his dad on that dismal day in June.

A couple of days later, as he marked off the dimensions of his father's grave and began to dig it, Cecil wondered why some of the men that Enoch had been so willing to help were not doing this last deed to help him. He was grieving the loss of his dad and was hurting deeply on the inside. At the tender age of sixteen, he confused the love of God with the inadequacies of men. On that desolate summer day in June, Cecil buried his broken, grieving heart along with his father's body, pledging vengeance against the Christian community that he felt had let him and his father down in their hour of need. It was at this time Cecil took his first drink and learned that alcohol could be a friend that would help to ease the pain. He became angry with God and would spend the next forty years "wandering in the wilderness."

Maudie anxiously greeted Cecil and Elmer with the news that Bethel was in labor and needed to get to the hospital. Cecil instantly forgot about being tired from the day's work and cold from the relentless rain. He knew he had to get Bethel out of there, and soon.

Bethel was beginning to have stronger and stronger contractions. The back pain was intense now, and she was sure it was not false labor. Cecil and Elmer made a packsaddle by locking their hands together and sitting Bethel between them. She held on with her arms around their shoulders. They went outdoors to find floodwaters were rising even higher than when they had come in from work. The access path to the highway was already under water. This was going to be no easy task. They carried Bethel through an alternate route to get to the car parked by the highway. Instead of going down the lawn, across a footbridge, and then up to the road, they had to backtrack around the ever-rising stream that surrounded them. Cecil and Elmer were both worried about the situation. They knew it would take a miracle for them to get Bethel to the hospital. They carried her in their handmade packsaddle up a hill, down a hill, over railroad tracks, up another hill, until finally they made their way to the car.

The men were exhausted. They were young and strong and were no strangers to hard work, but as they listened to Bethel's cries of pain and prayers for mercy, they worried that they might have to deliver the baby out there in the black night in the pouring down rain. Their determination to get her to the hospital went beyond human strength that night. It was as if some unseen force guided their path and gave them endurance to get her to the vehicle.

They drove the car to Holston Valley Community Hospital. Upon arrival, Dr. Honeycutt, Bethel's obstetrician, gave her medication to ease the pain, and as she was settling down from the excitement of the evening, she began to doze. The pains were still coming, but the intensity had lessened. To Cecil, she appeared to be resting well. He assumed it would be a long night and the baby would arrive sometime tomorrow. Bethel's first delivery had been a long, drawn-out process. He was sure this delivery would be the same.

Cecil and Elmer left the hospital around ten o'clock. The adrenaline was wearing off, and fatigue from the day's work and the evening's events took over. Cecil decided to go home and come back early the next morning and await the arrival of his second child. He would get a good night's sleep and be fresh in the morning.

Tomorrow would be too late, however. Two hours after he and Elmer left the hospital, at 12:26 a.m., Bethel gave birth to a six-pound, five-ounce baby boy. He was small … he was beautiful … he was perfect! Dark hair covered his tiny head. His back and arms too were covered with fine dark baby hair. This was something only a mother would notice as she examined every inch of her new baby. He looked to be a week old already. Bethel beamed with joy at the thought of a son. She loved Donna beyond words but secretly desired a son this time. This would make the perfect, happy family: Dad, Mom, Donna, and now this little boy. They would call him

Billy Wayne. The name Billy would come from Cecil, whose full name was Billy Cecil, and the name Wayne came from Cecil's nephew, Wayne, whom both Cecil and Bethel were very fond of.

Cecil would be so proud when he heard. Perhaps now, with a son who would look up to him, he would want to stay home more.

This is perfect, thought Bethel. This would complete their lives, and they could become the perfect family. They could get their lives back on track and go forward from here.

With so much hope for the future and a good ending to all of the evening events, she fell into an exhausted sleep. She dreamed of a better way, of a better life with Cecil. She loved him beyond the boundaries of reason, and now, she hoped that their marriage could be what it was supposed to be.

Bethel slept soundly with her dreams. She was oblivious to the rains still coming down outside. The storms of that night were, in some prophetic sort of way, indicative of the storms that were brewing on the horizon of all of their lives. This new baby, Billy Wayne, born in the midst of a storm, would grow to see storms as a way of life. To him, there would come to be something magnificent about the Appalachian sky when it flashed with lightning and rumbled with thunder.

Change was definitely on the horizon of Bethel and Cecil's lives, but they had no way of knowing just how significant those changes would be, nor could they have slept as soundly that night had they known.

- *Chapter 3* -

A Life to Bargain

Bethel was a young mother, but the recent condition of one-year-old Billy Wayne signaled to her that something was wrong. He had been running a low-grade temperature for a couple of days, and she knew that she should take him to see the doctor as soon as possible. She bundled her baby up to protect him from the chill that still lingered in the air from winter and headed off to Dr. Bruce Adkins's office. She was afraid something was wrong with Billy Wayne. Donna had never been this sick before.

Bethel could tell that Billy Wayne was getting weaker as the minutes passed, and she was relieved when she finally arrived at the doctor's office. Dr. Adkins laid Billy Wayne's small body on the examining table and began checking his vital signs. Bethel watched as an urgent, concerned look came across Dr. Adkins's face. He turned to her and told her that her baby was very sick and had fluid in his lungs. Billy Wayne had double pneumonia along with chicken pox, except he wasn't breaking out in the watery blisters on the outside of his body. The virus was attacking Billy Wayne's body differently from how it normally did.

Dr. Adkins told Bethel that Billy Wayne needed to be admitted to the hospital immediately. Bethel knew her baby was sick, but she had not anticipated *this*.

Billy Wayne was admitted to the hospital and immediately put on IV fluids for dehydration, placed in an oxygen tent for the pneumonia, and given antibiotics. Bethel sat by his bed both day and night, refusing to leave his side. She wanted to be there with him, no matter what happened.

Cecil came in the evenings after work and sat with his son and wife. He too wanted to be there with his baby. Things were touch and go with Billy Wayne. The doctors didn't expect him to pull through. Everything indicated that this baby would soon succumb to death. He was just not strong enough to fight what was attacking his little body. He was extremely dehydrated and was not responding to the normal dose of medicine. They would have to increase his dosage to give him any chance of survival.

Despite higher doses of medicine, Billy Wayne's condition worsened. The doctors ushered Bethel out of the room as they hurriedly worked over Billy's frail, limp body that was quickly losing life. He didn't seem to have anything going for him. His heart rate was falling, and his breathing was becoming shallow. Bethel could hear him wheezing from outside the door after the medical team made her leave the room. She was so scared that she might lose her baby boy. The one thing that every mother prays she will never have to endure, she feared, was coming to pass. Nothing Bethel could do at this point could make him any better. She felt so weak and helpless. Desperate, she began bargaining with God; she asked Him to take her life and save Billy Wayne's. Every wrong choice that Bethel had ever made began to come to the forefront of her mind. She somehow felt that all of her mistakes had something to do with her baby being so sick. She knew God must be angry at her, so she pleaded with Him to take her life and let Billy live. In her heart, that night, she turned her infant son's life over to God. She completely surrendered him to the One that she knew loved all children, in hopes that He might spare Billy's life.

Years later, God would remind Bethel of her prayers that night.

The doctors soon discovered that Billy Wayne was allergic to the high doses of penicillin they were giving him. He was immediately taken off the antibiotic and treated with other medications. He recovered, and after five days of treatment for asthma, Billy Wayne was released from the hospital. Bethel and Cecil were glad to be going home and taking their baby with them. This asthma episode with Billy Wayne was the beginning of an illness that would plague him throughout his childhood and into his adult life.

Dr. Adkins became a friend indeed to Bethel and Billy Wayne over the next few years, as he saw Billy weekly for his asthma. He often gave Bethel the medication that Billy needed without charge. Bethel and Cecil were separated much of this time, and she often had little or no money with which to buy medication or pay for doctor visits. She was very grateful to Dr. Adkins for his generosity and sensitivity to her situation.

Bethel and Cecil's marriage continued to deteriorate for the next year. They were both still very young, and the adjustments of marriage as well as caring for two small children had proved devastating to their relationship as husband and wife. Bethel's dream of the perfect family had become a foggy notion of something that would never be. She felt unappreciated by Cecil and trapped in motherhood without help. Cecil believed it was a woman's duty to care for the children while the man made a living. Accusations of infidelity were slung at one another frequently. Cecil would occasionally stop by a bar on his way home from work to have a beer with the guys. Bethel felt like he was getting some fun time while she stayed home with the babies. She resented him greatly for this. She wanted to be a good wife and mother, but she felt like Cecil knew the exact buttons to push that would send her over the edge.

But Cecil felt like he deserved a beer or two after a hard day's work. He never realized that stopping off at the bar was such a big deal to Bethel. His evenings with the guys became longer and longer, as he would avoid coming home to Bethel's nagging about his evenings out. Some nights he didn't come home at all. It was like some huge destructive monster had been set in motion to destroy both of their lives, as well as their marriage. Neither Cecil nor Bethel believed in divorce, so they stayed married despite their many differences. They were both unhappy and blamed one another for their misery. Each felt trapped by the shortcomings of the other one. Their lives were turned upside down by the lifestyles that they lived.

Cecil often found comfort in the company of his drinking buddies and in the arms of other women. Bethel too found a way to feel worthy and desirable by the attentions of other men. The lack of devotion they had to one another and to the marriage vow they had made before God would catch up with them both in the years that followed. Their infidelities would haunt them in a most painful way, but a deep-rooted value placed on the sacredness of marriage kept them from divorce. It was the 1960s, and divorce was more of an atrocity than infidelity, so they remained Mr. and Mrs. Cecil Arrington for many years to come, despite the fact that those vows had been broken.

- Chapter 4 -

Mountain Movers

When Billy Wayne was almost two years old and Donna was three, Bethel felt the weight of the world come crashing in on her. She was pregnant again, and thoughts of worthlessness began to prevail in her mind. She felt as though her life had spun out of control.

It was early spring 1965, and Bethel, Donna, and Billy Wayne were living in Wood, Virginia, near Ft. Blackmore. Their house was a remodeled chicken house located in a field behind her mother's house. She and Cecil were separated at the time.

There were so many things wrong in Bethel and Cecil's life, and she knew she could never fix them. Guilt and condemnation overcame her as she contemplated bringing another child into the world … a child that she felt unworthy to care for. She had worked out a plan in her mind to end it all. That day, Bethel swallowed poison and sat silently, waiting to die. She had decided that Billy Wayne and Donna would be better off if someone else raised them.

After swallowing the toxin, her mind began to race, as she considered the baby inside her. *What have I done? She thought. I have taken a life! I have taken an innocent life!* With that reality setting in and knowing that the overdose was already in her body, she became hysterical. Bethel picked Billy Wayne up in her arms and took Donna by the hand and walked as fast as she could down through the field to her mother's house. When Mary Belle saw her coming, she could tell that something had happened. She asked Bethel, "What is wrong?" Bethel told her what she had done, and Mary Belle immediately called the nearest hospital. They told her to bring Bethel in as soon as possible.

After checking Bethel out in the emergency room, the doctor determined that the baby wasn't hurt, but Bethel had to spend the next few days in the hospital. Her main concern, however, was not that she had damaged herself but rather that she had harmed her unborn child. She was relieved to know that the baby inside her was going to be okay.

When Bethel was released from the hospital, she returned home to face Donna and Billy Wayne, who were waiting on their mother. She looked at them and thought to herself again, *What have I done? You kids have a monster for a mom!* Donna and Billy did not know that their mother had attempted to end her life. They only knew that she was sick and in the hospital. They were so excited to see her when she finally did come home.

As Bethel looked at their concerned little faces, a new reality set in. She realized that Donna, Billy Wayne, and the baby inside her were all she had in life, but that was enough. No one would ever again make her feel the way she did the day she tried to end her life. She determined then that she would have her baby and be the best mother she could. She felt scared and alone. Hiding her fears along with the secret that caused her to contemplate suicide, Bethel rebounded from this episode of her life, fractured, but not broken. The baby she carried did not belong to Cecil and she had made a desperate attempt to cover up her sin by ending her life.

When she left the hospital, she and the kids went to stay with her parents. Because she and Cecil were separated, it was the only option she had.

Though they were living apart, Cecil and Bethel saw one another occasionally. They always brought out the worst in each other, even though deep down there was a love that neither of them could understand.

A few weeks later, on March 12, 1965, Randall Malcolm Arrington was born. Billy Wayne had just turned two, and Donna Lynn was three and a half. Bethel and Cecil were still separated, but they would soon be reunited.

In July, after Randy was born, they all moved to a small cinderblock house located in Speers Ferry, Virginia, close to Cecil's mother. The house sat deep inside the Appalachian Mountains that rose above the Clinch River. One had to cross the railroad tracks on a dirt road to get there. Maudie's house was located even further down that same dirt road that

Cecil and Elmer had carried Bethel out of the night that Billy Wayne was born.

In this small cinderblock house, Bethel and Cecil made another effort to be a family, but their attempt was short lived. The children were aware of the tension between their parents. It was here that Billy Wayne began to embrace storms with a peculiar interest. He would sneak to the back porch whenever he heard a storm approach and watch the lightning shoot across the black Appalachian sky while wrapped in a warm blanket. The magical way it lit up the whole mountainside in a flash stirred Billy's senses; he could see a power greater than anything he had known. Billy liked to ponder on things and figure them out, even as a young child. The illuminating whips of lightning and the thunder that seemed to roll on forever through the mountains revealed God to Billy at an early age. He knew it must have been dangerous to be watching from the porch, because Bethel would always drag him to a safer spot whenever she found him there. Her warnings could not dissuade his curiosity for this magnificent display of wonder and his intent on having front row seats to this grand display of light and sound.

In the spring of 1966, Cecil moved the Arrington family to Weber City, Virginia. They moved to a house in a more residential neighborhood, up the street and across the railroad tracks from a church by the name of Sally's Chapel. It was at this church that Billy attended his first Vacation Bible School. He made praying hand bookends that summer at Bible school and learned much about a man named Jesus.

After just a little over a year in Weber City, the Arrington's moved again. In July of 1967, they moved to 310 East Carter's Valley Road, 3rd Street North, Gate City, Virginia, near the Tennessee border. They did not stay here long, but eventually they returned and this would become the place the Arrington children called home. They loved this house. When summer ended, Donna began school at Weber City Elementary. Billy Wayne and Randy remained at home with Bethel. Billy dreamed of the day he could start school with Donna.

Another year passed. It was now late summer of 1968, and the family once again moved to another location. This move would take them back to the countryside, close to Bethel's mother. Their house was across the blacktop road and up a steep bank from Mary Belle's house. They called it Nannaw's house; it had been Bethel's grandmother's old house. Mary Belle could step onto her porch and look across the way and see Billy, Donna, and Randy playing outside their house. Billy developed a strong bond with his grandmother during their time here.

Billy Wayne loved to go and visit his Granny. Often, he would sneak off from his house and make the trip over the steep embankment, across the road, and down the drive to Granny's. When Bethel would realize what he had done, she would be very upset and threaten to switch him when she got hold of him. Granny would holler up to Bethel's house and ask her to let Billy stay with her longer and not to whip him. Billy felt safe with Granny on his side. She, too, catered to Billy Wayne. He was an affectionate child and showered Granny with hugs and kisses of appreciation for the things she did for him. Little and frail as he was, she loved to feed him in her attempt to help him grow stronger. A huge pot of pinto beans was always cooking on the stove and a fresh pan of corn bread was always baking in the oven. Billy knew he was welcome there. He felt a sense of belonging when he was with Granny. She told him Bible stories and sang hymns. She would take him to the garden with her to gather vegetables for the yummy meals she would cook. He helped her gather eggs and feed the chickens.

On occasion, unbeknownst to anyone else, she would sneak him a cup of coffee. Billy felt special in sharing not only the chores with his Granny, but also their secret about drinking coffee. He could trust her. Granny taught Billy the love of God just by the way she lived her life and the way she welcomed him into her home. Once, she gave Billy a glow-in-the-dark cross. He took it home with him, and night after night, when all the lights were out, he would look at it until he fell asleep. He knew it was important and it should be respected, but at such a young age, he did not fully comprehend the enormity of the cross, but even then … God was watching.

Life with the Arrington family was always full of surprises. One night, after the kids had gone to bed, Cecil brought home a goat and quietly made a bed for it in the closet of Billy's bedroom. Cecil thought it would make a nice pet for the kids. When Billy woke up the next morning, he discovered his dad's gift and was thrilled to have a pet goat. As the goat grew, it became more bothersome than Bethel could tolerate. It ate and chewed on everything in sight. She had finally had enough and gave the goat to the neighbors who lived down the road. A few days later, Bethel heard that the neighbors had eaten the goat for dinner. She regretted giving it away then and would not have done so had she known they were going to be serving their family pet for dinner. She kept this news from the children, knowing they would have been upset.

There was a room in the back of Nannaw's house that held some items left over from the former tenants. One of the leftover items was a record player and an old record of "Pop Goes the Weasel." Billy Wayne was five years old, and he found much delight in entertaining anyone who would lend him their eyes and ears, and especially their applause, as he danced to and sang "Pop Goes the Weasel." Donna enjoyed his entertainment almost as much as he enjoyed being the entertainer. Billy could always count on Donna to be a good audience; he could always make her laugh.

Christmas came along that year, and Mary Belle and Bethel's sisters Beverly and Carol were busy putting on a Christmas play at the Wood Riverview Baptist Church. Bethel and the children attended the church as often as they could. They loved being there with their Aunt Beverly, Aunt Carol, and Granny. Although Bethel and Cecil were not separated at this time, their stormy relationship was still chaotic. On the night of the Christmas program, Mary Belle, Beverly, and Carol came to the house and begged for Donna and Billy to be little angels in the program (Randy was too young to participate). Bethel didn't have anything for them to wear, but in desperation, and wanting the kids to be in the play, her creativity kicked in and she pulled white sheets from the closet and made halos from the tinsel off the Christmas tree. Billy and Donna went to church that night and sang as little angels. Aunt Beverly stood on a stool with a white dress that flowed down to the ground, and all the children sat around her and sang Christmas carols, dressed as little angels. Billy, at his young age, was struck by the splendor of the whole scene. It was here, in a little country church deep in the Appalachian Mountains of western Virginia, that Billy became awed by the power of theatre. It was a night that he would never forget.

- *Chapter 5* -

Loving the Unlovable

In the autumn of 1969, Billy Wayne and his family moved back to the little farmhouse in East Carter's Valley. This house was located about one-fourth of a mile below where they had lived previously at 310 3rd Street North. While living here, Cecil's nephew, Larry Bledsoe, came to live with the family. Larry was the son of Cecil's sister, Evelyn, and he was in his early twenties. Cecil had secured him a job where he worked at Grief Brothers, and it was more feasible for Larry to live with Cecil and his family than to drive the thirty-some miles from where he lived to get to work. Billy and Randy had bunk beds and shared a room with Larry. He came to be like an older brother to Billy. Moving Larry into the house seemed like a good idea at the time but soon proved to have disastrous results.

This would be the year that Billy Wayne began first grade at Weber City Elementary School. He had anticipated this day for as long as he could remember. Billy was still very small, and in fact, he was the smallest boy in his class. This is something a young boy notices when he is in a room full of other boys. The children all checked one another out the first few days of school. They already knew who was the prettiest, the poorest, the biggest, and the smallest.

Despite Billy's small size, his world would soon collide with that of the biggest boy in the class, Dobie Darnell. Dobie came from a very poor family, and an unpleasant odor followed him wherever he went. He had difficulties learning to read and write, and quickly fell behind the rest of the class. Most of the children made fun of Dobie because he was different.

No one wanted to be seen hanging out with him. In the eyes of all the children, Dobie was a real loser. Billy Wayne was no different than the others. He didn't want to be seen with Dobie either. Dobie was someone to avoid because he simply wasn't pleasant to look at, nor did he smell very good. It would certainly be difficult for a young boy or girl to look past the physical appearance of someone like Dobie long enough to become friends with him.

Billy Wayne was the opposite of Dobie in most ways. He was little, limber as a dishrag, and smart. Though Bethel couldn't afford the best clothes for her children, she always made sure they were neat and clean. On the first day of school, Billy Wayne's teacher, Mrs. Margaret Mays, gave all the children a book with which they would learn to read. It was *Tag*, a big red book with a black Scottish terrier on the cover, and Billy was excited to read it. He was a fast learner, and he quickly mastered that first book and progressed to the *Dick and Jane* books. He felt quite good about himself and his accomplishments. His teacher often commended him on his zeal for learning and his enthusiasm to participate. Each positive comment made him want to try even harder. Mrs. Mays was so confident in Billy's learning ability that she asked him to help another student in their first grade class. That student turned out to be Dobie Darnell. Billy was not happy about the situation. Now, everyone would think that he was friends with Dobie. The thoughts of sitting next to Dobie made Billy feel faint. What would his classmates think?

Billy wanted to do what Mrs. Mays expected of him. He reluctantly secluded himself in the back of the room at a table with Dobie and began reading aloud to him. He couldn't help being concerned that the rest of the kids would think he and Dobie were best friends. Billy was humiliated to be in that situation.

He half-heartedly tried to help Dobie sound out the words, all the while darting a quick glance at the rest of the classroom to see who might be watching.

In the *Dick and Jane* series, there was a dog named Spot. The first lesson was a simple paragraph that read: "See Spot. See Spot run. Run, Spot, run."

Dobie would try and try to sound out the words. His first attempt was feeble. Dobie read, "Sssssseeeeee … Sssssdog."

Billy would interrupt, "Does that word look like 'dog'? It starts with an 's.' Try again." Billy wanted Dobie to learn more quickly so he could rejoin the rest of his classmates.

Time after time, Dobie's attempts to read proved futile. Billy became frustrated, but after a while, he got used to being identified with Dobie and decided that he wouldn't give up. For each day that he sat with Dobie, the fear of what others were thinking was replaced with the desire to accomplish his task. Billy resolutely continued teaching Dobie by pointing at the words as he read. Then, finally it happened. Dobie got it right!

"Sssseeee Spppot. Ssssseeee Sssspot rrrruuuuun. Run, Spot, run!"

Billy could not believe his ears. Dobie was reading! You go, Dobie! You did it!

From that day on, Dobie was no longer seen as a big, stupid reject. To Billy Wayne, he was a person and he had feelings. The other kids in Billy's class would no longer be able to make fun of Dobie when Billy was near.

Billy hadn't wanted to sit by Dobie and tutor him, but God had other plans. Through the humiliation of having to work so closely with someone such as Dobie, God taught Billy a lesson that would last a lifetime. He taught him that everyone has worth, and given the chance, even someone like Dobie has something good to offer the world.

Billy also became acquainted with Camilla Horn that year. Camilla rode the same bus to school as Billy. Everyone made fun of her. She was overweight and had psoriasis. As with Dobie, none of the kids wanted to have anything to do with her, including Billy. Billy would stay clear of Camilla for now, but eventually, God would see to it that their worlds would collide.

As soon as that school year ended in 1970, the Arrington's moved to Mitchell Mill Road in Ford Town near Colonial Heights, Tennessee, just outside of Kingsport. Bethel was pregnant, and after a summer of getting settled in to their new home, she gave birth to her third son, Gerald Ray, on August 25, 1970.

This move meant that Billy Wayne and Donna would be attending a new school in the fall: Miller Perry Elementary. Billy was unhappy much of his second grade year because he missed his friends back in Weber City Elementary. He developed a crush on his second grade teacher, Mrs. Stafford, but then he began to fear that her husband would find out about his secret. With this fear, the romantic notion faded.

After school, Billy spent much of his time in the field behind the house in a huge, old black cherry tree. The house they lived in was old, and there was no inside bathroom or running water. The Arrington children took their baths on the back porch in an old metal tub. There was a hand pump in the kitchen for drinking water and an outside toilet in the pasture behind the house. Ill-behaved horses that grazed in the field often made a simple trip to the outhouse a major chore. Billy Wayne didn't much like this place, except for the old black cherry tree that provided a safe place for a young boy to hang out and think about what the rest of the world was doing.

During that winter, Billy Wayne and all of his siblings fell ill with the measles. It was a difficult year for everyone. Billy's asthma continued to be bothersome, and with four children in the house, Bethel was often exhausted. She and Cecil remained married, but in name only.

It upset Billy to see his mom and dad fight. He saw the things they were doing and would sometimes tell them what he thought. To Cecil, who was raised to respect adult authority regardless of the consequences, Billy Wayne's outspokenness was rebellion. Cecil felt that Billy Wayne had a bad attitude and was hard headed, and he thought that Bethel only fueled his stubbornness by giving in to him all the time. When Cecil would try and explain this to Bethel, she would reiterate that Billy Wayne was just like his father. Cecil found it easier to avoid Billy Wayne than to be a father to him.

On July 7, 1971, the Arrington family made a final move back to their dream home at 310 3rd Street North. After having moved so many times, this was definitely their favorite place to live. The house had indoor plumbing and sat in East Carter's Valley, which was the most beautiful place to live in the area. The hills rolled up from the valley, and the meadows and fields seemed to go on forever. The house was located in the country, but unlike all their other homes, it was fairly close to the city. It was bigger than any other house they had ever lived in, and there were three porches on it, which made the Arrington children feel like they were living in style. Now, finally, they would settle down in something that belonged to them. After all the years of renting, Bethel, now pregnant with her fifth and final child, at last convinced Cecil that buying this house was in their best interest and that renting was just a waste of money. Just a few weeks after moving into this house, Bethel gave birth to Shannon Scott on August 11, 1971.

Shortly after the move back to the dream house, Billy Wayne, Donna, and Randy began going to church at Tabernacle Baptist Church on Bloomingdale Pike in Kingsport. The church had started a bus ministry to pick children up for services. Billy, Donna, and Randy started going to church regularly because of the influence of David and Ida McGee and Joe and Carol Crawford.

The first time Carol ever saw Billy Wayne was at a church-sponsored activity for the local elementary school children. Billy was sitting on the steps, crying. There had been a family crisis, and he was very upset. Billy's burden for his family started at a very early age. Carol talked with him that day and encouraged him in the Lord. Almost instantly, Billy developed a respect and admiration for Carol that would serve as a personal example of how to be a Christian who reaches out and helps others.

Billy was very faithful in his church attendance. He became a vital part of the church's youth program. At "Super Saturday," a church-sponsored activity at Greenland Park, Billy Wayne became quite the entertainer for the rest of the group. He did cartwheels over and over. There was always a group of adults close by applauding his efforts and encouraging him to just be himself. He was also the clown and told stories. Everyone's favorite was a comedy skit that Billy performed called the banana and handkerchief story.

Billy Wayne impressed the adults who led the youth group because he was so dependable at such a young age. The young people had to earn their own money for the many trips and activities they participated in, and Billy never shunned his responsibilities. Carol and Joe thought of Billy Wayne as one of their own family. They could see that he had a vision of who he wanted to be and was determined to reach his goals by using his talents to glorify God, no matter what obstacles he had to overcome.

Not long after he began attending Tabernacle Baptist, Billy heard the gospel message that would eventually come to be the entire focus of his life. He rode the bus every Sunday and learned songs about Jesus. He would also learn a Bible verse each week. God was hiding His word in Billy's heart for the future. One Sunday morning, Pastor Cecil Sturgill was preaching a message on the fiery pits of Hell, and Billy knew he didn't want to go there. He went forward, and the pastor prayed for him. He wasn't sure of all that was happening, but he knew that he wanted what the people at this church had. This was the beginning of Billy's spiritual journey. He was baptized a short time later.

Granny Salling and Mammaw Maudie Arrington were very encouraging when it came to Billy's walk with the Lord. They stood behind him and cheered him on in his faith. Granny Salling became a rock in his life, and he loved going back to the mountains and visiting with her at least one week every summer for many years to come.

The move back to 310 3rd Street North allowed Billy Wayne to go back to Weber City Elementary School, where his friends were. He began third grade there in the fall of 1971, with Mrs. Lessie Blackenbecler as his teacher.

Billy had a deep desire to attend church. He was very vocal and demanding to both his mom and dad that they should go to church also. Billy thought that he had a duty to make his parents feel guilty for not going, which he tried to do often. He knew that his parents were not living like God wanted them to live, and his sharp words would cut deep when he reprimanded them. They didn't want to hear it from their child. Billy didn't follow their rules, but here he was, at eight years old, expecting them to follow his. His sense of righteousness at an early age, coupled with Cecil's lack of it during that time, drove a wedge between them that would only be driven deeper over the next few years. Cecil needed no one, especially his child, telling him what he was doing wrong. He knew all too well what a mess he had made of his life, and he didn't need Billy Wayne or anyone else to remind him.

Other people who knew Cecil and Bethel would offer unwelcome advice to Cecil about how he should be raising his children. They would often tell him that he was too lenient with his kids. Cecil got more advice than he could follow about child rearing. Some people even went so far as to tell him what time he should make his kids get out of bed in the mornings on their summer breaks. Supposing that everyone else could see his failures only made him feel more like one. Alcohol dulled the overwhelming sense of failure, as did other things. In Cecil's mind, God had turned a deaf ear to his cries, but that was okay because he wasn't crying anymore. The alcohol made sure of that.

As young Billy watched his mom and dad fight and saw how discontented they both were, he determined in his mind to live a happier and better life than his parents. He was young, but he decided that he would navigate his own way through life. He would not end up like them. They made him sick. God must have made a mistake by putting him in this family. Billy began crying out to God to give him a good family, one that would love each other and not scream and curse at one another.

For Billy Wayne, school was a refuge from the life he hated at home. At school, he could be who he wanted to be. It was as though Billy was living a double life: the life he lived at school, where teachers complimented him and he could excel, and the life he lived at home, where he learned to tune out the adults in his life. He craved praise from his teachers and found great joy in going above and beyond what he was supposed to do to receive their approval. Billy loved being the best at whatever he did at school. At home,

Billy had become a loner. He would spend countless hours by himself. He had heard so many fights between Bethel and Cecil that he turned a deaf ear to both of them. Bethel would tell Billy to do his homework, and he would sit in front of the TV and act as though she had said nothing. This frustrated Bethel greatly. He would do the homework on his own time schedule. She would not control him as she tried to control Cecil.

At home, life in the Arrington household regressed from bad to worse. Cecil and Bethel fought most of the time. Often, Cecil would disappear for a solid week. Bethel begged Cecil to take her and the kids on a vacation: away from their home and the situations that had been created there. She told him they didn't have to go anywhere special or do anything special, just be together.

Cecil responded to her, "Oh Hell, y'all gonna just nag, nag, nag, bitch, bitch, and bitch."

Both Bethel and Cecil had done things they couldn't forgive themselves for at this point. Their relationship was so estranged that they never had a good word to say to one another.

Problems had developed because Larry was still living in the house. He and Bethel were close in age, and he was there for Bethel when Cecil wasn't. Cecil found comfort outside of the home, and Bethel, with five children to care for, found it in Larry, who was already there with her. Bethel knew that her relationship with Larry was not good, and she asked Cecil to make Larry leave. Bethel knew that Larry was the biological father to two of her children, but he had become more of a burden to her than a comfort. Larry was another person for Bethel to look after and care for. She hadn't wanted things to go the way they had between her and Larry, and now she wanted him gone. Cecil wouldn't ask Larry to leave, even though he knew he was having an affair with his wife. Perhaps by turning a blind eye to what was going on between Larry and Bethel, it lessened the guilt Cecil would have otherwise carried because of his trysts with other women.

Billy Wayne knew something was going on between his mom and Larry. He had, on occasion, witnessed Larry and Bethel being intimate, but in his young mind, he was very confused about what he saw. Once, Larry and Bethel were going to a drive-in movie, and Donna, at age twelve, was babysitting her younger brothers. Billy, trying to make sense of what was going on in the lives of his mother and Larry, tested the waters by taunting Larry with the question, "Are you going to kiss her?"

Billy's question outraged both his mother and Larry. Larry spanked Billy for saying that, and Bethel told him never to make such comments again. Billy showed much disrespect for his mama during this time. He loved her, but she confused him. Once again, young Billy Wayne questioned God about being in the wrong family. Surely God must have meant to put him in a family with parents who could get along with each other. Life was supposed to be wonderful and happy. Other parents loved their kids and didn't do the things that his mother and father did. Other fathers didn't drink, and other mothers didn't have boyfriends.

Billy felt a great injustice had been delivered to him in the form of his parents. He felt sorry for himself at times and at other times he felt self-righteous in that he was trying so hard to live a Godly life. He had every right to point out his parents' mistakes to them. God would be proud of him for doing that, because they didn't seem to know on their own.

Cecil experienced yet another loss in his life with the death of his brother, Elmer, at the young age of twenty-one. The Arrington brothers were as close as brothers could ever be. They had always worked together and played together. There was an unbreakable bond between them and a love that ran as deep as the mountain ravines they lived in. They took care of one another through thick and thin, and nothing could sever their ties. When Elmer died, Cecil knew that his brother was the father of Randy. It had happened during a time that Cecil and Bethel's marriage meant no more to them than a piece of paper. Cecil would step up to the call of being a brother to Elmer by being a father to Randy. He would love Randy as his own, and there would be no need to tell him any differently.

At the same time Bethel was pregnant with Randy, another woman was carrying Cecil's child. That child would be named Billy Jr. Neither Cecil nor Bethel could blame the other for being unfaithful. They had both been unfaithful to a vow that had gotten lost in a sea of carelessness. Their disregard for their marriage vows was a reflection of their lives that had gotten far away from serving God. Both Bethel and Cecil had made a profession of faith in their lives, but they had turned from God and back to lives that searched for fulfillment in the things of this world.

Where had life taken the first wrong turn for them? Everything had started out just the way it should in the life of a young couple. The first time they ever met was in church. In 1958, going to church was as much of a social affair for younger people as going to the local drive-in theatre. Bethel sang as part of a duet that night, and Cecil admired her from the congregation. She was so full of life, and he was smitten as he watched her sing. The words that came from her mouth were closer to heaven than anything he had felt for a long time. *Surely this is how an angel looks and sings,* he thought. Their courtship was short, and after eight months, they secretly ran away and eloped.

When they were first married, they lived with Cecil's mother, Maudie Arrington. Evelyn and Raleigh Bledsoe, Cecil's sister and brother-in-law, had given them seven acres of land. Bethel was so excited when she and Cecil were able to buy furniture for their first home. For $500, they purchased a dresser, a bed, a mattress, and a chest of drawers, along with a dinette table with six chairs, a cast iron coal stove, a refrigerator, two end tables, two lamps, a couch, chair, three new rugs, and curtains. There was so much hope for the future then. Somewhere, somehow, everything changed.

Bethel's first inkling of Cecil's infidelity came while she was pregnant with Donna. He boarded away from home during the week, as Bethel stayed at home. When he was home one weekend, Bethel was cleaning out his pants pockets. She began looking through his wallet. What she found was only the beginning of the troubles that would plague their marriage. There were pictures of another woman in Cecil's wallet. Bethel's heart broke. Those pictures confirmed Bethel's fears. Something inside of her died that day.

God would remind them both of their commitment to Him in the years that followed, though. Would they ever return to a life of serving Christ? Perhaps they would, but not without many regrets.

Billy's sister Donna mothered him on the rides to and from school. She was only two years older than he was, but Billy Wayne had an uncanny knack for finding trouble. Because he was so determined to be his own person, it led to some unsettling times for him, as well as for Donna.

The bus rides were as traumatic for her as they were for Billy Wayne. Because he was so small, the older boys found him easy prey. Since they could always get such a rise out of him when they taunted him, it was almost a daily chore for Donna to keep him from getting beaten up. Billy Wayne felt a lot bigger than he actually was. No one on the bus was going to tell him where to sit or what to say. He didn't fear what the older boys might do to him. Billy had been subjected to volatile situations at home so much that he wasn't going to back down from confrontation in any other area of his life. Donna would plead with the older boys not to hurt him because he was so little. She would practically have to sit on him to keep him quiet on the bus. Her daily prayer became, *Oh Lord, please just let Billy*

Wayne sit down today and shut up. Billy became determined at an early age to take charge of his own life and not let other people, especially kids, tell him what he could do and how far he could go with it. God began honing that attitude and continued to do so in the years to come.

Billy found favor with Donna's girlfriends. They all loved him because he was so little and attentive to them. Billy Wayne loved the way the girls included him. He loved learning things from them and hanging out around them. They made him feel important. Donna didn't mind because he wasn't mouthy with her girlfriends like he was with the boys.

As Billy and Donna continued going to church and hearing the Word of God, he began to learn the difference between right and wrong in God's eyes. He knew drinking was wrong, but his father did it. He knew cursing was wrong, yet both his parents did it. Billy wanted better parents—parents like Joe and Carol Crawford or David and Ida McGee. Here he was, going to church and trying to be a good boy, and his parents were not going to church, nor were they trying to be good. Billy developed a spirit of self-righteousness that further drove a wedge between himself and his parents.

The next school year was fourth grade, and Billy Wayne's teacher was Mrs. Melda Starnes. She was tremendously encouraging and didn't mind being involved in the lives of her students. She would run and play basketball with the boys, and her humor was equally matched with her love for her students. She wore a wig, and once, while on the court, her wig became loose and fell to the floor. She never missed a step as she swooped it up and snapped it back over her scalp, all the while focusing on the game at hand. That day, she taught her students about being a good sport in the midst of a potentially embarrassing moment. Without saying a word, they all learned something.

All of the students had to do physical fitness exams that year. Billy could do everything in the exam with ease, but the 600-yard dash run/walk was a nightmare for him because of his asthma. Even most of the girls could outrun him. Halfway around the field, Billy Wayne's chest heaved as he gasped for air until he finally fell to the ground and passed out. Mr. Carter, the gym teacher, had to work with him to get him to breathe again. The rest of the class all stood and watched. After Mr. Carter revived Billy Wayne, he was told that he would have to finish the run so his time could be recorded. Mr. Carter had to help him across the finish line. Billy Wayne was embarrassed and humiliated by the whole situation. He could do more sit-ups and pull-ups than all the other boys, but because he couldn't run the 600-yard dash, he was labeled as a weakling. The 600-yard dash was a devastating giant to Billy that he was determined to conquer someday.

Billy continued going to church regularly and learning more about the Lord as Bethel and Cecil continued to argue and fuss. Initially, Bethel encouraged Billy to go to church, but eventually she would stop encouraging him in that area. His religion and faith in God was cramping her lifestyle, and she didn't want to hear about it from him.

Billy would get aggravated at his parents and Larry. They all partied together, and they thought it was funny to give Gerald and Shannon beer in their baby bottles. Billy voiced his opposition and was often punished for speaking out against their actions.

Being the oldest boy, Billy Wayne felt that he fell short of everything Cecil wanted him to be. Cecil was an avid sportsman in hunting and fishing, and he spent much of his time, when not at work, fishing on the river banks or hunting in the woods. Billy learned how to shoot everything from a pistol to a sawed-off double-barrel shotgun, and he could fish as well as anyone, but he just didn't have an interest in doing those things the way Cecil would have liked. Billy was more artistic and enjoyed performing backyard plays with his cousins, Terry and Deborah, or singing. Hunting just didn't interest him. Though Billy Wayne wanted a relationship with his father, their differences created a huge gaping tear that would not easily be mended.

Bethel referred to her children as Donna, Billy, and "the boys. Cecil would take the boys, Randy, Gerald, and Shannon, hunting and fishing, and leave Billy Wayne and Donna at home. Billy was more interested in attending church services on Sunday morning than going hunting. Cecil would tell Donna and Billy that they were ruining their plans for the day by going to church. He knew that Billy didn't like hunting and fishing. Oftentimes the boys came home from hunting with small toys and candy that Cecil had bought for them. Billy knew that there would be no toy or candy bar for him. This caused resentment to grow in Billy toward his brothers, especially Randy. At school, teachers sometimes openly compared Randy to Billy Wayne. Randy was a slower learner than Billy had been, and even Bethel sometimes blamed Billy because of the teachers' comparisons. Billy and Randy had personalities that clashed, and the natural human emotion of jealousy ran its course daily in the household.

Billy was reaching the point of giving up trying to win his father's favor. He felt hopeless and worthless. *If Daddy doesn't think I'm worth much,* he thought, *I surely must not be.* "You god damn son of a bitch, you'll never amount to anything." Those words cut like a knife as Billy tried to win Cecil's favor. Billy was too young to understand that a dad should not talk to his son that way. He had no choice but to believe his father's words. They cut deep and they hurt, but he loved his father anyway.

As badly as Billy wanted a father/son relationship with his father, he found himself more and more at odds with him. Billy defended Bethel when arguments broke out. This caused Cecil to push Billy even further away, and a seed of resentment continued to grow between Billy and Cecil. They had no idea what kind of a monster would emerge from this tiny seed of bitterness. Billy would continually attempt to win his father's approval, but to no avail. No matter what Billy Wayne did, it never seemed to be good enough. He longed to hear his father say, "I love you and I'm proud of you." Billy couldn't ever remember Cecil saying that to him.

As Billy became more opposed to Cecil's drinking, his anger with his father grew. Cecil was an avid fan of wrestling on TV. Billy hated watching it. One Saturday morning, Cecil and Larry were watching wrestling with their six packs of beer in the living room. Billy came through and accidentally knocked over a bottle of beer. Cecil grabbed him and got him in a leg lock and wouldn't let him go. He started punching Billy on his arm and told him that he needed to toughen up and be more like a man. Billy Wayne screamed that it was hurting and begged his father to let him go. Cecil had a few beers in him and he decided he was going to make his son tough. He didn't want to hear Billy's whining and got all the more angry with him. He began to pound Billy's arm harder and harder. Billy knew better than to cry too loudly. If Bethel had heard what was going on, she would have come to Billy's aid, and it would have erupted into a fight between Bethel and Cecil.

Billy was finally released from Cecil's clutches. He made his way to the kitchen, out of sight, to examine his arm. His small, fragile arm now sported a goose egg-sized lump, and it was red and swollen. He was hurting, but he couldn't let anyone know, so he cried silently. Billy's attempt to hide it failed as his mother walked into the kitchen and saw him applying ice to his arm. The fight between Bethel and Cecil occurred despite Billy's efforts to avoid it.

The Arrington children could not remember a day without Bethel and Cecil fighting out loud. The kids each learned ways to diffuse the conflicts that would erupt around the house. Donna always had a special way with Cecil. She was a daddy's girl and always brought out the best in him. She loved her father. He was a good father to Donna.

Everything that Billy was learning at the church was just the opposite of what he saw at home. He was grieved as he watched his parents fall into sinful lifestyles and prayed that they would change. Though he still didn't understand everything about being a Christian, he knew that he wanted his family to know Jesus. He went to the altar regularly and prayed for them … and he knew that God was watching.

- *Chapter 6* -

Becoming a "Somebody"

Growing up in the early 1970s in the foothills of the Appalachian Mountains of southwestern Virginia, there wasn't much organized entertainment for children. Billy Wayne and Donna played mostly with their double first cousins, Debora and Terry Arrington. Cecil's brother Howard had married Bethel's sister Berniece. Debora was the same age as Donna, and Terry was the same age as Billy. The Arrington children became the directors of their own plays, the chefs of their own mud pie bakeries, and judge and jury of all their disagreements. With both sets of parents living beside one another, the four were destined to become best of friends.

Billy Wayne was the organizer of the group, although he was younger than Donna and Debora. He would set up the stage area with sheets on the clothesline and was usually the director and the star of the show. The girls played along with him because of his skill in putting together a good show. They performed their own rendition of *Romeo and Juliet* and other plays, and old clothes stored away from past proms and formals became great costumes. The foursome would practice their plays till they had them perfected, and then they would campaign for an audience consisting of their mothers and Mammaw Maudie. Maudie had given up housekeeping by this time and would travel between the homes of her different children; she spent a lot of time at Berniece and Howard's. Though Berniece and Bethel spent much time socializing, drinking coffee, talking, and reading the newspaper, Maudie always had time to be the undistracted audience for whom the children loved to perform. She also taught the children much by her unwavering, confident faith in God. She read her Bible every day and seemed to have profound wisdom. As Billy learned from her example, he desired to possess the qualities he saw in her that made him feel special.

The four Arrington children developed a strong bond that would last a lifetime. They spent their days together, as well as their nights. The four were inseparable. Through good times and bad times, they knew they could always count on one another. They seldom had a disagreement.

Sunday morning was an extra special time to the foursome, as the church bus always picked them up and took them to church. Neither set of parents went to church at that time. Billy, Donna, Terry, and Debora sometimes dreaded the visit of the bus ministry people on Saturday afternoons to encourage them to attend Sunday morning worship, but by the time they got home from church Sunday, they were always glad they had gone.

The ride on the church bus took about an hour. It was during this time they learned lots of memory verses and songs; it was a time that would impact their lives forever.

Billy Wayne was in fifth grade that year, and his homeroom teacher was Mrs. Lowell Culbertson. Mrs. Culbertson demanded each student's best efforts in her classroom. Though her expectations were high, she was equally ready to give praise when she saw a student excel, which is exactly what Billy Wayne was becoming an expert at doing. He was beginning to find a way to escape the inadequacies of childhood and his life at home. If there were someone who believed in him, then he would prove himself worthy. He wouldn't let anyone's expectations of him bring him down, the way he had been let down so many times. He would show his parents that he did have worth. They would see, and then they would love him and respect him. Billy desired this one thing, which seemed most out of reach, more than anything else in the world.

He often thought that if his parents would come to church, then they would be a happy family. His desires to see them come to know the Lord were tainted by his own desires to be accepted by them. This resulted in him praying relentlessly to see his parents saved in a way that would benefit him. Billy prayed that prayer for that reason for many years.

Sixth grade proved yet another challenging year at home, while school continued to be the only place where Billy Wayne could excel.

He had made the big trip up the hall of the school from the "kiddy end" (grades K to five) to the "happening end" (grades six and seven), with Mrs. Sue Slemp as his homeroom teacher. Ms. Helen Jayne Wolfe was his language arts teacher that year, and she immediately fell in love with Billy Wayne's enthusiasm to learn. He took a seat in the front row, closest to the door (perhaps planning an easy escape if things didn't go exactly the way Billy expected). He wore a bright red shirt that would barely button across his chest and light blue jeans that failed to meet the tops of his socks when he sat down. He was squeaky clean with an adorable cowlick and a smile that could only be described as electric. Ms. Wolfe often said that if the power had gone off, they could have plugged in Billy and continued with their studies. He was a delightful student to have in her classroom.

Ms. Wolfe was a wise teacher and felt that if she provided the proper motivation for her students, they would learn. She would begin each class by leveling the playing field. This she did by imagining each student was a blank piece of paper and hoping they would give her clues as to what they would like to write there. The clues she got from Billy, however, wouldn't have fit on a football field.

Billy, his classmates, and Ms. Wolfe spent that sixth grade year, as well as Billy's seventh grade year (after he landed a spot in Ms. Wolfe's homeroom), growing together. She taught them grammar, punctuation, spelling, parts of speech, composition, vocabulary, literature, listening, creative writing, acting, and speaking, as well as cooperation, responsibility, the work ethic, adventure, and thinking about possibilities. Ms. Wolfe had to work even harder than the students did just to stay even with them.

Knowing there were problems in Billy's home life and seeing the potential he had, Ms. Wolfe encouraged him in every area. Billy Wayne adored her. She saw all the things in him that were good. Those two years, she nurtured all of his positive attributes and helped him prune the negatives. She was astounded at how he refused to let the negative aspects of his life overpower the positive. In Ms. Wolfe's classes, he would try anything, volunteer for everything, and do a superb job each time. Meanwhile, many things were taking place in Billy's life during his seventh grade year. He was still riding the bus to Tabernacle Baptist Church with Donna, Terry, Debora, and Michelle, who was Debora and Terry's younger sister. Donna and Debora were old enough to attend youth group meetings, and Billy and Terry couldn't wait to turn twelve so they could go as well.

Randy had stopped going to church. By this time, the bus ministry was flourishing at Tabernacle, and many different workers were helping with the bus routes. Tabernacle was a wonderful church that did an excellent job in outreach and evangelism. It was an independent, missionary Baptist church that tended to lean on legalism at times, but the gospel message was always presented. Unfortunately, compassion and grace were sometimes forgotten. The church had so many rules—do's and don'ts—that it was often hard to keep up with what was sin and what wasn't. Depending on the youth minister at the time, it was or wasn't a sin for girls to wear jeans. Women were discouraged from wearing pants. The guys were expected to keep their hair cut over their ears and off their collars.

This was okay for Billy and Donna, because the blessings of being loved and learning about Jesus far outweighed the rules and regulations. It wasn't the same for Randy.

One particular Sunday, the bus came to pick up Billy, Donna, and Randy to go to church. Billy came out in a buttoned-down shirt and a pair of khakis. Donna was wearing a dress that Bethel had bought at a bargain store. Randy came out dressed in a t-shirt and blue jeans. One of the bus helpers asked him to go back in and change clothes. The truth was, this was all Randy ever wore, unless he borrowed something from Billy.

Donna and Billy waited patiently in the bus while Randy went back inside the house. In just a few minutes, Randy appeared back in the doorway, tears running down his face as he waved to the bus to go on. Donna and Billy were upset as well but just assumed that Randy had decided not to go. It was the last time Randy would ever go to church during his childhood. He felt he wasn't good enough for church or God. Bethel and Cecil told him that he would never have to go back to church again if he didn't want to. When Billy and Donna returned that afternoon, they were told that they could not go back to church again if the people there were that fussy. Even though Billy and Donna felt bad about Randy, they wanted to keep going to church.

After much convincing and prayer, Bethel and Cecil allowed Donna and Billy to continue attending church. The children would often make deals with their parents in order to go. They would work in the garden, mow the lawn, and do extra work in turn for being allowed to attend church. They learned early that following Christ comes at a price.

In October of Billy's seventh grade year, he attended a youth revival at Tabernacle Baptist Church. Billy Bernstein was the evangelist, and he doubled as a ventriloquist. Billy Wayne was amazed as Bernstein spoke. He had attended on Friday night and was drawn in immediately by Bernstein's way of sharing the gospel. He couldn't wait to get back to the church on Saturday night. At that time, Billy Wayne could not have foreseen how his life would be changed on that Saturday night.

He returned to the revival on Saturday night and was anxiously waiting to be entertained by Billy Bernstein's message. The evangelist began the sermon, and after a few words, Billy Wayne could hear something else. God was speaking to his heart. As a matter of fact, God was speaking more loudly to Billy Wayne than Billy Bernstein was speaking from the pulpit. God spoke clearly that night as he held Billy Wayne captive to His voice. For the first time, Billy understood that he was a sinner and that Jesus died for him—not just the whole world! Yes, Billy remembered going forward when he was seven years old, and he remembered not wanting to go to Hell. He could recall Pastor Cecil Sturgill praying for him, but he couldn't remember ever calling on Christ and praying himself. He couldn't even remember asking for God's forgiveness or asking Jesus into his heart. Beyond the shadow of any doubt, he now knew that God was speaking to him about that. He understood that he was the sinner that placed Jesus on the cross. Billy's desire was for Jesus to live in him and be absolutely surrendered to the Lord.

He sat there while God whispered his name and urged him to make a decision. In his mind, Billy didn't want to go forward. Everyone thought that Billy was already a Christian. He was already helping out in the bus ministry and going on visitation with the adults on Saturdays. He attended church every Sunday, and he was a part of the youth group. What would everyone think? Would they think he had been a liar? Would they trust him now?

For Billy to walk forward and admit that he had been "playing church" would be humiliating. He would have to swallow his pride. God's voice spoke even louder, and Billy yielded to the call that night. He went straight to the church altar, bypassing the preacher. This night would be between him and God. He had read the parable in Luke 15 of the lost sheep. Billy knew that night, that the Shepherd had left the ninety-nine sheep in the open country and had gone after the one lost sheep. When He found it, He picked it up joyfully and brought it home. Billy was that lost sheep and God was calling for him.

That night when Billy called upon the Lord, admitted his sin, and asked Christ to come into his heart, Jesus joyfully picked him up and carried him into the presence of God the Father and said, "Look, Daddy, I brought him home." All the angels in Heaven rejoiced and partied in Billy's honor. It was the greatest day of his life.

Billy Wayne was so overjoyed with what had taken place in his life. He couldn't wait to go home and share the good news with Bethel and Cecil. Their only comment was, "I thought you had already done that."

Ms. Wolfe will be excited for me, he thought. Monday morning couldn't come soon enough for him to share his newfound joy with her.

He was right. She was elated with joy for him. She told him that God had great plans for his life. He believed her. She saw something special about Billy and never missed an opportunity to cultivate what she saw growing. Billy had won a leading role as the husband in the class drama, *Foxy Grandma*. He had been bitten by the theatre bug. Standing before audiences and hearing their approval was something that was almost addictive. Making people laugh and seeing them forget about their problems for a while was something Billy loved to do.

From that point on, people began to see a big difference in Billy. It was no longer about church and religion. It was about a relationship with Jesus that had changed his life forever. His boldness gave him joy but would also bring him many struggles as he stood for what was right.

It was a big year for Billy Wayne. He was becoming a somebody. He ran for king in the fall festival. It was to help raise money for the school. People rallied around Billy and helped him win by raising the most money. He was amazed and humbled at what was taking place in his life. Before this, he felt unworthy. Life at public school was great now.

Being inspired by Billy Bernstein's ventriloquism, Billy Wayne asked for a dummy for Christmas that year. He got one and was quick to learn the art of ventriloquism. He entered art contests for the state and won. He began to get involved in 4-H and ended up winning the Share-the-Fun talent show for the district. He had the opportunity to go on and compete at the regional level, but his parents failed to see the importance and did not allow him to compete.

Before the school year was over, Bethel had to go into the hospital for emergency gall bladder surgery. Billy was quite upset at school that day. Ms. Wolfe took him to the office and let him call long distance to the hospital to talk to his mom. His teacher had become a great mentor and friend. She also instilled in him a love for the English language and writing. He would greatly miss her when he moved on to Shoemaker Junior High the following year.

As Billy led the seventh grade graduation program for the parents, student body, and teachers in the spring of 1976, Ms. Wolfe was very sad, as she knew she was saying good-bye to Billy. She said a prayer for him and turned him over to God, confident there would be teachers at the next level who would see the promise, initiative, and talent she had seen in him. If he had to take ten steps to everyone else's one, she knew he would continue to work hard, filling up that blank piece of paper that was the size of a football field.

- Chapter 7 -

Bullies and Compassion

In 1976, our country celebrated two hundred years of independence. It would also be the year that Billy Wayne would declare his own independence.

Bethel and Cecil's relationship had grown more estranged due to Cecil's alcoholism, and their marriage was severely damaged from years of neglect by both of them.

Bethel had started to work as a cook at Lynn Garden Restaurant, which gave her a sense of independence and a belief that she possibly could do something about her marital situation. At this point, Cecil was rarely home. Billy Wayne and Donna were old enough now to see that the marriage was not going to work, and they often encouraged their mom to divorce their dad. They had witnessed too much in their young lives, and it was time for a change. With Bethel working, much of the care and responsibility of the three younger children now fell to Billy and Donna.

Both Donna and Billy had newspaper routes, and they saved their money for youth trips and church functions. With five children in the house, an allowance was not an option.

Billy Wayne was in eighth grade now, and it would prove one of the hardest years of school that he would ever experience. Several seventh grade classes from across the county came together at Shoemaker Junior High School. It was the largest eighth grade class the school had ever seen. All of the familiar faces and friends Billy had made in elementary school were shoved to the background as new faces took center stage. Billy was still one of the smallest students in the whole eighth grade class, and he felt swallowed in a sea of so many people. Once again, he would bear the brunt of everyone's tormenting. His relationship with God had grown by this point, and he knew he had a friend in Jesus when he didn't have anything else. Aside from his friendship with Jesus, the only other friend who understood him was his cousin Terry.

Billy was constantly being bullied by the bigger boys, especially the athletic jocks. Two of Billy's worst nightmares were Ronnie Begley and Jack Anderson. They were always picking at him and taunting him. They would knock his books out of his hands and trip him going down the steps of the school building. They seemed to find much delight in making his life miserable. Billy was often humiliated by scenes like this, which only served to deepen his feelings of low self-esteem.

There was also a girl, Edna McDavid, in Billy's gym class who was also a bully, and she liked to intimidate everyone. She always had sidekicks around her who would cheer her on. Every day, it seemed as though Edna fought with someone. It must have been her way of boosting her own self-esteem. Billy knew to stay out of her way. She was definitely trouble, and he didn't want any of that.

Billy's relationship with Jesus continued to grow. While the others participated in sports and were busy being kids, God was doing a great and mighty work in what appeared on the surface to be one of the weakest students at the school.

> *"My grace is sufficient for you, for my power is made perfect in weakness." 2 Corinthians 12:8 NIV*

As Billy searched for significance in his life, God was etching His Words in Billy's heart. When the world told him he wasn't important, God's Word confirmed that he was. He chose to listen more closely to what God was saying. Carrying his Bible to school with him every day made him a target for insensitive bullies. Edna seizes the opportunity. She began calling him "Jesus Freak" long before dc Talk wrote the song. Knowing that he wasn't ashamed of his belief in God, she tried all the harder to tear him down. Billy would ignore her as best as he could and continue reading his small New Testament Gideon Bible.

Shortly after Billy had been saved, he and Terry decided to hold each other accountable. They rode the school bus together every day. They would memorize Scriptures, sing Christian songs, and encourage each other in their faith walks. Terry was a strong Christian and loved the Lord with all her heart. They even shared a paper route together. Living next to each other made it easy to stay close and accountable. Once, a silly disagreement kept them separated for about a month. Terry's parents had agreed to allow some of the kids from church to come home with Terry and Debora to spend the night. Billy Wayne and Donna were among the invited. At one point in the evening, Terry and Billy started to argue about where Terry's mom had gotten her new clock; Terry claimed that her mother had won it in a card-punch game. Billy protested that she hadn't won the clock, but that someone had given it to her. Their words got heated and louder. Billy got so angry that he ended up pushing Terry backwards and knocking her down. Uncle Howard sent Billy home and reprimanded him for knocking Terry down and speaking harshly to her. Billy and Terry eventually reconciled their friendship, but not without a period of separation in which they missed each other's company.

Gym class became a real hassle for Billy Wayne. He felt very awkward and never big or strong enough to compete with the other students. One day, on his way to gym class, he went downstairs as always to dress out for gym, which was a requirement. He hated to get dressed in front of the jocks. To Billy, it seemed as though every other boy except himself was magically sprouting muscles. He remained skin and bones. He felt as though every eye was upon him. It was a humiliating experience every day. On this particular day, Billy made his way down the rickety steps to the basement of the gym. When he hit the bottom step, he knew something was wrong. The floor was flooded with inches of water. All of the guys, including Ronnie and Jack, were standing around laughing. Billy ignored them and went straight to his basket where his gym clothes should have been. All of the baskets were locked, but someone had pried his basket open and had taken his clothes.

Billy heard Ronnie taunting him, "What's wrong, Billy? Did you lose something?"

Jack chimed in, "You might want to look in the toilet."

Billy went over and sure enough, there were his clothes clogging the toilet. Water was overflowing and filling the concrete floor. Most of the other guys joined in laughter. A few who were sympathetic said nothing, in fear of being targeted by the bullies. Billy was humiliated, to say the least. He got his clothes from the toilet and wrung them out. He had nothing else to dress in for gym class and was afraid of having his grade docked by the coach.

Billy said nothing to Ronnie and Jack, but proceeded upstairs to tell the gym teacher what had happened. He didn't mention anyone's name in fear of more ridicule. The teacher was very unsympathetic. He told Billy that he wouldn't dock his grade this time, as long as he still participated; but if it happened again, Billy's grade would be docked.

A few weeks into the school year, it was time once again for the physical fitness examinations. All through elementary school, Billy was never able to successfully master the 600-yard dash without passing out, due to asthma. Each year, he felt complete humiliation because he could never finish the run. He wanted it to be different this year. He wasn't afraid of any of the tests except the 600.

In memorizing Scripture, Billy came across a verse that really ministered to him; it would be a verse that would change his life this particular school year. It was Philippians 4:13: *"I can do all things through Christ, which strengthens me."* What a verse for the underdog, and Billy had enough childlike faith to take God at His Word.

The day finally came around for the 600-yard dash. Billy was nervous. He didn't care about coming in first. He only wanted to give his best for God. He wanted to finish the race without any assistance and hoped to finish before some of the girls. This time when he went up to the starting line, something was different. Billy kept reciting in his mind, over and over again, *I can do all things through Christ, which strengthens me.*

When the whistle blew, Billy was off. He wasn't looking at anyone around him. He imagined Jesus at the finish line, waiting for him. He could hear the Lord whispering to him the whole time he ran, "Billy, you can do it. I am here with you." He kept reciting Philippians 4:13 in his thoughts. His chest began to fill with air. He started wheezing a bit. He slowed himself to his own pace and listened to the Lord's voice. His heart was pounding. His lungs were burning and aching. He could see the finish line. Runners were passing him. He tried not to concentrate on anything but the finish line. Repeatedly, he told himself, *I can do all things through Christ … I can do all things through Christ.*

As Billy Wayne crossed the finish line that day, he felt as though all of heaven was rejoicing for him. He took God at His Word. Christ was his strength, and he had finished the race for the first time in his life. He had even finished before some of the girls and a couple of the guys.

This verse and this triumph in Billy's life inspired him to take a stand against some of his greatest fears that school year. He had been praying for an opportunity to confront Ronnie and Jack. One day, he felt that God was giving him the chance to do just that.

The Shoemaker Junior High building was ancient and soon to be torn down. The lockers did not have doors or locks. There were only shelves for students to put their books on. One day, Billy went to his locker to get his biology book, and it was missing. Someone had stolen it. He looked throughout the day at other people's books to see if he could find his. Finally, he saw his book. There it was, cradled in the arms of none other than the bully he feared, Jack Anderson.

Billy was determined to say something about his biology book and to confront the pair, regardless of the consequences. He had withstood all he could endure from them, and he knew that God was on his side. He felt like David against two Goliaths, but he knew where his strength would come from. Billy entered the school early the next morning before classes started and walked right up to the two bullies.

"I want my biology book back," he said. "I know you have it. It's in your hands right now."

Ronnie and Jack began to laugh. "What are you going to do about it?" Ronnie asked, as he poked Billy hard in the chest.

Billy dusted himself off and walked up to them both again. "You stole my biology book, and I want it back right now!"

"What are you going to do about it, wuss?" asked Jack.

"If you don't stop messing with me, I know somebody who's gonna mess you up," Billy replied without hesitation.

"Bring 'em on! We'll meet 'em after school. We're not afraid of anybody or anything," they chimed together.

With all power and confidence, Billy proceeded, "I am a child of the living God. Jesus lives in me, and if you don't stop messing with me, He's gonna mess you up."

Ronnie and Jack stood in silence. There was a long pause. Ronnie and Jack exchanged glances as if to get a clue from the other of what to say or do next. Neither spoke. Ronnie dropped his head and slowly pulled the biology book from his cradled arm and handed it to Billy Wayne. "Here's your book, man. Sorry." Both Ronnie and Jack then walked away.

From then on, those guys seemed so small to Billy Wayne. They were always very polite to him. The greatest victory came in tenth grade, when Ronnie came to Billy and asked him to pray for his mother, who was very ill and in the hospital. He said to Billy, "I know that you are a Christian. My mother might not make it. I know that if you pray, God will listen." Although Billy and Ronnie never became close friends, they had a great respect for one another.

The next obstacle was Edna. Billy had no idea how God would work that situation out. Little did he know, God already had a plan.

One Friday while delivering papers on his paper route, Billy was collecting fees. As always, he would spend time with his customers. One of his favorite customers was Mr. Salyer. Mr. Salyer was a Christian and loved to talk about Jesus when Billy had the time to chat. Before Billy left Mr. Salyer's home that day, he asked Billy a question that surprised him. "Billy, you go to Shoemaker Junior High in Gate City, right?"

"Yes, sir," Billy replied.

"Do you know Edna McDavid?" Mr. Salyer asked.

Billy did not know what to say. He was hoping that Mr. Salyer wouldn't ask him what he thought of Edna. "Yes, sir, I know Edna. Everybody knows Edna," he replied.

"She's kind of rough, isn't she? You might not know this, but I am her grandfather. I try to tell her about Jesus, but she's pretty rebellious. She doesn't want to hear about the Lord. Would you do me a favor?" Mr. Salyer asked.

Unsure what his request would be, Billy hesitantly answered, "Sure, Mr. Salyer. Anything I can."

Mr. Salyer proceeded, "I want you to agree with me in prayer that God will save Edna. Pray for the Lord to work in her heart."

"I'll do it," Billy replied.

Billy couldn't wait to get back to school on Monday. After gym class, he went to the top of the bleachers and began reading his small Bible. Like clockwork, here came Edna, along with her sidekicks.

Edna shouted toward Billy, "Hey Jesus Freak! You're a Jesus Freak!"

Billy calmly responded, "Edna, come up here a minute. I want to talk to you."

Edna was evidently puzzled by Billy's request. Looking inquisitively at Billy, she, along with her sidekicks, made her way up the bleachers to where he sat.

"What do you want?" she asked.

"You really think I'm a Jesus Freak, don't you?" Billy asked.

"Yeah, you're weird man, you're weird," she answered. Her sidekicks chimed in and laughed.

Billy intently responded, "Well, Edna, if I am a Jesus Freak, then so is your grandfather. Mr. Salyer is a wonderful man of God. He loves you. He wants you to know Jesus too. He asked me to pray for you to know Jesus as your Lord and Savior. Jesus died for you and wants a relationship with you. Edna, I am going to be praying for you that you will come to know Him someday."

Edna was perplexed by Billy's comments and slowly turned and made her way back down the bleachers.

From that day on, Edna never said anything negative to Billy. Her life was on a collision course with God, and some years later, she accepted Jesus as her personal Savior.

In the spring of 1977, near the end of the junior high school year, God would teach Billy one of the greatest lessons he would ever learn. No Christian can ever be truly effective until he or she learns about true compassion.

While riding the bus home from school one day, God made Billy's heart feel compassion toward a fellow student. Camilla Horn had been picked on every day of her life since first grade. Billy could remember people always picking on Camilla. Every day, when she got on the bus, no one would let her sit down. She was forced to stand in the aisle and hold onto the seats and her books at the same time during the bumpy bus ride.

Conviction started in Billy's heart one day. God began to show him that he needed to befriend Camilla by letting her sit with him. He argued with God in his heart that if he let her sit with him, then all the other kids would think that he loved her.

God simply asked Billy, "Well, don't you?"

This was a real eye opener for Billy Wayne. God had pierced his heart. Billy looked around the bus at all his peers and looked at Camilla, who was standing and crying in the aisle.

"Camilla," Billy said, "come and sit down with me."

All of the other students started laughing and chanting, "Billy loves Camilla."

"Yes, I do, and so does Jesus! Do you have a problem with that?" Billy blared at the students.

No one else said anything. Every day, Billy and Terry would save Camilla a seat on the bus if they got there before she did. Through their conversations, they found out that she was a Christian, too.

Camilla would not live to see her twentieth year class reunion. She would die prematurely of complications with diabetes. She had suffered much in her life, but her rewards are now in heaven. Maybe, because of a shared seat on a bus, Camilla knew someone actually loved and cared for her.

During the summer of 1977, Billy attended drum lessons at Gate City High School. He made the marching band, ended up going to band camp at the school, and was selected to play the triple tenor tri-toms for the Big Blue Marching Band. He would spend his summer preparing for the upcoming marching season.

The Lord began to place some wonderful people in his life at this time. One particular person was Karen Richards Patrick. She was truly a woman of God. She took Billy, Donna, Debora, and Terry under her wing and began to show them Jesus in a way they had never seen. She became Billy's spiritual mother and mentored him. She showed him unconditional love and acceptance.

Often, she would pick Billy up and bring him to her home and let him vent. She never judged him or his family and always gave Godly advice. At the time, no one knew how instrumental she would become in Billy's life and ministry, but in the future, she served on the executive board and worked for his ministry of Vision Productions.

As Billy Wayne became a freshman at Gate City High School in Gate City, Virginia, he also became more involved in his youth group at Tabernacle Baptist Church in Kingsport, Tennessee. The two towns were very close in distance, though they are separated by state lines.

Billy was learning some valuable lessons from God at an early age. He was a natural-born giver, much like his father, Cecil. Though Cecil wasn't the best of fathers at times, everyone who knew him loved him. It sometimes confused Billy to see how respected his father was by others, all the while living with him as an alcoholic. Cecil was a compassionate man and would often give money to poor people on the street. Billy and Cecil shared more traits than either of them would have admitted.

One Sunday evening at church, Charles Fields, a missionary from Managua, Nicaragua, was sharing his testimony and trying to raise support for his work. God began to prompt Billy's heart. Billy only had ten dollars left from his work on the paper route. He used his money to buy things he wanted or to attend youth events. Many times, people in the church would see the need in Billy's life and help him financially, but he couldn't rely on that happening. He needed some money of his own in his pocket. That night, God prompted Billy to give all he had to the missionary. He had never felt so strongly about obeying God as he did that night. As the offering was passed, Billy laid his last ten dollar bill in the collection plate. He had no idea what he would do for money for the rest of the week, but he was sure he had obeyed God.

Immediately after the service, someone in the church came to Billy and handed him one hundred dollars. Billy stood in shock. The person said that God told them to give Billy that specific amount.

Billy experienced the joy of giving and trusting God that night. He learned that obedience is greater than sacrifice. He knew from that point on that God would always supply his needs as long as he was obedient to God's voice.

There were so many blessings and lessons in Billy's life that year from God, yet the one thing he desired more than anything else—a better relationship with Cecil—only grew more remote. They became increasingly estranged as the days passed by. Billy gave up on seeking Cecil's approval in his life. The already widened gap between father and son grew, and soon Billy conceded that he really had nothing in common with his dad, and perhaps never would.

- *Chapter 8* -

Pull the Trigger

It was the bitter cold eve of the coming new year of 1978. So far, this was proving to be one of the coldest winters on record. Bethel had left the house earlier in the evening to go to a New Year's Eve party at the Veterans of Foreign Wars that she and Cecil had planned to go to together. Earlier in the day, Cecil had been drinking and broke his foot while driving a motorcycle. He insisted that Bethel go ahead and attend the party without him, while he stayed at home with the kids and rested his foot.

Like every other holiday Billy could remember, Cecil was drinking alcohol. Because of his broken foot, he was also taking prescription medication for the pain. Sometime during the evening, the mixture of pain medications and the Jack Daniels whiskey took its toll not only on Cecil but on the entire Arrington family.

As Cecil sat at home, tending to his injury, a friend stopped by and told him that Bethel was having a good time at the party dancing with other men. The cocktail of whiskey and pain medication spoke to Cecil of his wife's actions. He could no longer control the anger that was building inside of him. His mind began to fill with jealousy and rage. The longer he thought about it, the angrier he became.

Billy and his two youngest brothers, Gerald and Shannon, lay snuggled and sleeping on the living room floor in front of the television. They had been watching "Dick Clark's New Year's Rockin' Eve" until they all fell asleep. Randy was also asleep, slouched in a chair with his feet hanging to the floor. Suddenly, Billy was awakened by an enraged Cecil, who was threatening to kill Bethel. Billy could hear his mother's car, a Grand Prix equipped with a cherry bomb muffler, nearing the house as she returned from the party. Billy could tell that there was something different about Cecil's drunken state that night. He truly believed that his father would kill his mother if he didn't act fast.

Billy jumped up and ran outside to warn his mother of the impending danger and to tell her to get back in her car and leave. When Bethel saw Billy's distress, she assumed something terrible had happened inside the house. She imagined the worst: that someone inside was hurt and needed help. As she bolted from her car to make a mad dash to the front door, she tuned out what Billy was saying. Cecil jumped off of the front porch, broken foot and all, and met her before she could get to the door. His hands found her small neck as the rage continued to build inside him. He was applying pressure, and Bethel was afraid he would kill her. The rest of the children were awake by now and screaming for Daddy to please stop hurting Mommy. Randy ran to the neighbors' house to call the police. In his excitement, he ripped their storm door right off the hinges and broke the glass trying to knock loudly enough for someone to hear him. A call to the police went through, but could they get there in time?

Bethel struggled to free herself from Cecil's death grip. She herded the two younger boys inside the house to protect them from the cold and from Cecil. They were wearing only their underwear because they had been in bed when the fighting broke out. Once she was inside, Cecil wasn't far behind her. He chased her with a vengeance, despite his broken foot. Bethel headed to the back door to escape from the chase she was sure would end in violence if Cecil caught up with her. Billy Wayne watched in fear. It seemed as though the whole world suddenly stood still and silent, as if he were watching a scene from a horror movie in slow motion. He watched anxiously as Bethel fumbled with the dead bolt on the back door, trying make her escape. Fear raced through Billy as he silently prayed for her successful escape through the door. Every detail, every word became amplified a thousand times in Billy's mind, like a split-second accident when everything shifts into slow motion but you cannot do anything to prevent it.

Bethel's fingers finally worked the deadbolt in the right sequence to allow her to escape. She headed toward the neighbors' house as she fought off Cecil's attacks. She knew there was something dreadfully wrong with Cecil that night. This was unlike his usual drunkenness. She was exceptionally afraid. Billy ran outside behind his parents in an attempt to somehow defuse the escalating violence that was unfolding before him and his brothers. As he watched his mother slip and slide on the ice in her high-heeled party shoes, while attempting to escape to the neighbors' house, Billy could see that his dad was going to catch up with her even as he struggled with a broken foot. Next, he saw her on the ground and Cecil on top of her, punching her with his fists. Billy could hear his younger brothers, who were standing on the front porch, screaming and pleading for Daddy not to hurt Mommy. Reacting instinctively to their pleas, Billy attacked Cecil with all his might in an attempt to save his mom. Cecil did not even notice that Billy was hitting him. It was the first time Billy could ever remember hitting his dad. How could the scene five minutes earlier of Billy and his brothers sleeping so soundly and peacefully have turned so bad, so quickly?

Cecil finally got off of Bethel, dragged her by the hair to the other side of the road, and slammed her head against a neighbor's truck. As abruptly as he had attacked her, he left her alone and went back into the house. Billy hurriedly helped his mother and his younger brothers into the car. Then he noticed that they didn't have any clothes on. He ran back inside the house to get clothing for his brothers, because the night was bitterly cold.

Billy found Cecil had ransacked the closets and drawers in the house. Clothing was strewn all over the floors. Billy grabbed a few items of clothing and left the house. When he got back to the car, he noticed that his mom had taken off her coat with a fake fur collar and wrapped it around Randy's arms because they were cut badly from the broken glass at the neighbor's house.

Bethel and her children sat in the car, waiting for the police to come. Cecil, not feeling any pain in his foot, made his way back out to the car. Billy's window was cracked as Cecil began to shout at him. He demanded that Billy unlock the car doors and get out. Billy refused. Cecil barked to Billy that he had ten seconds to get out of the car or he was going to blow his brains out. Just then, Billy noticed that his dad had a gun in his hand.

Many thoughts ran through Billy's mind during those ten seconds. Billy always thought he would be frozen with fear if a gun was ever pointed at him, but instead he had a peace that passes all understanding. Jesus began to speak to Billy's innermost being: "Billy, you are my child. I will work this out. Everything will be all right no matter what happens."

At that moment, Billy looked into his father's eyes as tears streamed from his own and said, "Daddy, go ahead and pull the trigger. I am a child of God, and I know where I'm going." Then he braced himself for a bullet. He expected to hear a shot ringing through the dark night, ending his life. He knew Cecil was not in his right mind and believed that he was capable of killing him that night.

No bullet was fired—no shot rang out. Instead, Cecil went to the other side of the car and tried to get to Bethel. She begged for Cecil to let the boys go and she would do anything he wanted. Cecil said, "No, we're all going for a ride." Because he had a broken foot, Bethel was able to push him away and drive off.

Tragedy was avoided on that frigid New Year's Eve in East Carter's Valley. Riding down the road, Billy had forgotten how cold it was till now—now that they were out of harm's way. Recalling the surreal evening, he rode quietly in their escaping car. The stinging chill of that frozen winter night returned and the hot tears that had earlier run down his face now made his cheeks cold. There were so many unanswered questions. Uncertainty became the only reality as they drove away into the night.

- Chapter 9 -

Seeds of Bitterness

It was life as Billy Wayne knew it. Each holiday and birthday became just another occasion for Cecil and Bethel's already volatile marriage to escalate into the kind of feuding that affected the whole family. Billy grew increasingly bitter as he watched his parents ruin the days that should have been times of celebration. He was developing a strong sense of justice and would freely speak his opinion, often at the expense of others' feelings. Donna often became angry at Billy for his strong words and failed to see Cecil's abuse from Billy's perspective. She was still daddy's little girl, and Cecil somehow managed to control his mood swings around her. Both Donna and Billy had become Christians early in their lives. Donna had a tendency to find the best qualities in people and overlook their inadequacies, yet Billy's nature was to point out such inadequacies and address them. Donna and Billy occasionally had disagreements because Billy was so obstinate and condemning of their parents. Both children wanted to see their parents accept Christ, but Donna's approach at pointing them toward God differed from Billy's. She believed her parents would come to know Christ if she overlooked their faults and loved them unconditionally. Billy, on the other hand, truly believed they would come to know Christ only if they could see what was wrong in their lives, and he was all too willing to show them. He had been hurt many times by their thoughtlessness, and he felt no remorse in vigorously trying to prove that he had been right about so many things along the way.

Many Christian people spurred Billy along as he developed a strong spirit to stand firm for God. As far as Billy was concerned, though, his parents were ungodly heathens. His words to them lacked love and respect and were often filled with condemnation. Billy had taken a legalistic standpoint where his parents were concerned, and he considered them not only unsaved but possibly even unworthy. Both Bethel and Cecil knew that Billy was right, but neither would allow his self-righteous behavior to change their lifestyles.

A pivotal day came in May of 1979. Billy and Donna came home from school and told Bethel they needed to discuss something with her. Billy was now sixteen, and Donna was eighteen. Donna was engaged to be married to Tony Williams at the time, and the children thought it necessary to sit their mother down and tell her of a decision they had reached. They explained to her that if she didn't divorce Cecil, they were both going to leave home. Bethel was devastated. She had contemplated divorce many times but had never actually gone through with it. She and Cecil were estranged, but she had grown accustomed nonetheless to their marriage just as it was. It had come to the point that they fought every night, keeping the children awake. Every weekend was a huge blow-up between Bethel and Cecil, sometimes involving the children. After some consideration, Bethel agreed that Billy and Donna were right. The lives of all involved would be better without Cecil. Billy and Donna had high hopes of experiencing some normalcy in theirs and their younger brothers' lives with their father absent.

Bethel immediately began the process of filing for divorce. One day when Cecil came home for lunch, Bethel cooked him a meal. After he ate, she laid the divorce papers on the table in front of him and said, "Here's your dessert."

He looked at the papers, and after realizing what they were, he laughed and said, "Who in the Hell wants a woman with five kids?" Cecil knew they never had been the perfect family, but he had never expected that Bethel might divorce him. He didn't show up at court on the day of the divorce hearing. It was over. The explosive marriage between Cecil and Bethel Arrington ended on July 20, 1979. Cecil later commented to some of his friends that on that day, he lost *everything*. Once the marriage was dissolved, he realized what he had done and tried to regain what he had lost. He always paid his child support on time, but he and Bethel never reconciled.

Bethel and Cecil went their separate ways, but troubled times remained for the Arrington children. Bethel was still working evenings, and Billy and Donna had full responsibility for the care of their three younger brothers.

Bethel leaned forward toward the mirror to get a closer look at the make-up she had applied. She slightly touched the curve of her lip to push the lipstick back in place. Donna stood behind her, helping her fix her hair.

Billy Wayne was watching from across the room. He knew his mama was going out tonight. He had never liked seeing her dress up to look beautiful for the men that would be at the dance halls and the bars. Watching her transform herself from a mom into someone that would attract men grieved Billy tremendously. He wanted Bethel to be the mother she had once been to him and his brothers and sister—the mom who had taken the time to hand-sew him a Halloween costume when they had no money. He yearned for the mom who had put popcorn in plastic baggies with twist ties on the front porch for the other trick-or-treaters when there was no money to buy candy.

Billy's brothers were still young and needed their mother at home. Resentment toward Bethel and her nights away from home was mounting up in Billy's heart. As she liberated herself from her motherly duties, she passed the burden on to Donna. Bethel knew Donna would take good care of the boys while she was away. Being a kind, gentle-spirited person, Donna took the responsibility without question. She didn't approve of her mother's actions, but she would take care of her brothers without much complaint. In face, she was already used to taking care of them due to Bethel's work schedule at Lynn Garden Restaurant.

Bethel reasoned that Billy and Donna were responsible teenagers who took excellent care of the younger children. Shortly after Bethel and Cecil divorced, Donna married Tony and moved out. She still felt a strong sense of responsibility for her younger brothers and also to Bethel, but at the same time, she longed for a life apart. Now, most of the childcare responsibilities fell to Billy Wayne. It was now even more difficult for him to stay after school for extra-curricular activities since this would leave the boys alone. Billy could only imagine what it must be like to hang out with friends from school like other teenagers. He would hear the other kids talking about the things they did after school on their own time, like going to the mall. Billy Wayne wondered how it felt to be carefree, and he missed having a normal teenage life. Everything inside of him ached to act like a normal teenager—to spend countless evenings laughing and hanging with the guys, or maybe even to sit at a movie and eat popcorn with a girl. He resented the responsibilities that were forced upon him. Billy was so embarrassed about his situation that he could never even bring himself to speak of it to any of his friends. He dreamed of the day that life would free him from the family responsibilities that had fallen to him. Someday, Billy Wayne Arrington would make his own choices.

Unlike Donna, Billy Wayne openly resented those responsibilities. Billy loved his brothers, but he did not want to be a substitute parent. He cooked supper for them in the evenings, did their laundry, and cleaned up after them. After supper, he would run his paper route and then return home to help the boys with their homework, get their baths, and put them to bed.

For Billy, life at home was overwhelming at times. Reports reached social workers that Billy was taking care of his younger brothers while his mother partied at all hours. They needed Billy's testimony, and the social workers questioned him in front of Bethel. Billy avoided answering their questions. The social workers returned later and told Billy they needed his testimony against his mom so they could provide help for him and his brothers. Billy's main concern was keeping the family together, but he was informed that, more than likely, no one would take all four of them into the same home. Instead they would be split up and placed in separate foster homes. Billy therefore refused to testify. He wanted and needed help, but not at the expense of losing what was left of his family.

During this, Billy's darkest hour, God sent him an "angel in the flesh." Her name was Ruth Hensley. Ruth and Bethel had been best friends for many years. Both of their husbands had been outdoorsmen, which had brought them together many times. They were as close as any sisters could ever be and shared the most intimate secrets. It grieved Ruth to know that Bethel had become less of a mother than she should have been. She loved Bethel but became very concerned for the children. Often, she would find herself going by the house to check on them. She kept this from Billy and would act as though she were only there to talk with Bethel. Ruth became like a surrogate mother to Billy. He adored her as if she really were his mother. She had stepped into Billy's life and had become what he needed when Bethel was shirking her duties at home.

There were times when Billy and Ruth would follow Bethel when she went out. Bethel had a history of dating abusive men, and the two self-made detectives became close confidants in their quest to watch out for someone they both loved. They always hurried home so Bethel would never know they were spying on her.

Because of all these things, Billy never dated. There was no time for it. Although he was popular with the girls and treated them with respect, he had no confidence to approach them for a date or any kind of relationship other than friendship. Because he did not date, he was often accused of being gay. Billy tried as best he could to ignore the rumors. They were hurtful, but even so Billy was outspoken about his virginity and stressed sexual purity even in high school. He ended up taking his close girlfriends to his proms and banquets. Donna Bishop, Joanna Argo, and Tammy Fields were three of those friends who always seemed to be there for him.

Billy did develop feelings for one particular girl, although. He had a crush on K. C. Quillen. She was one of his best friends in the world, and in the midst of all the chaos at home, she became a comfort for him at school. Every morning when he arrived at school, he would seek out her face to be comforted by her smile. K. C. never knew how her humor and friendship helped Billy to make it through the rough times that he hid from most people. As much as Billy wanted more than just friendship with her, he felt he couldn't take the risk of losing her friendship by pursuing a relationship. They shared something far too special, and Billy wasn't willing to endanger that. In Billy's mind, it was best to leave well enough alone. In his mind, he didn't feel worthy of someone as wonderful as K. C.

Billy's only social activities were playing in the band at football games and activities at church. He never spent the night with anyone from school. He was at the point where he was ashamed of his family background. At times, he felt trapped. It was not until he began planning to attend college that he felt his life would improve. Entertaining the thought of college became a ray of hope for his future.

Christmas of 1979 was an extremely difficult holiday for Billy's family. Bethel didn't want the kids to see Cecil's family, and she and Billy got into a huge argument, and she threw Billy out of the house with his suitcase. He went to his aunt's house and was tracked down by Bethel. She threatened that if he didn't come back home, she would have him put in a juvenile detention home. Billy purposed in his heart not to be bitter toward his mom, and he prayed for the Lord to keep him from hating her. The Lord granted his request.

Accordingly, Billy knew that hating his father was wrong. The divorce had been a wake-up call for both Billy and Cecil. In fact, it had relieved much of the tension from their relationship. Cecil now realized how much he had lost, and he began trying to make up with all the children, including Billy.

Billy wanted a healthy relationship with his father more than anything, but at times, thought there were too many bad memories to start over. He finally became honest with himself and the Lord about how he felt toward his father. One night, at age sixteen, Billy began to cry out to the Lord with the truth of how he felt in his heart. "I hate him! I hate him! I hate him!" Billy was being brutally honest as he prayed. "I don't know how to love him! Teach me how! Love him through me!" He cried out to God from the depths of his soul with his deepest needs. Billy realized that, try as he may, he could never love his dad or forgive him in his own strength.

From the time he was seven years old, Billy prayed for his parents to be saved. He realized now that all these years of prayer were for selfish reasons because he secretly desired his own life to be easier. He knew that there was a long road of forgiveness ahead, but for the first time, Billy sincerely wanted to mend relations with his father. God began to work a miracle of forgiveness in his heart toward his dad. Growing up, all Billy ever wanted to hear from his dad were the words, "I love you, and I'm proud of you." He desired that affirmation and approval from Cecil from the depths of his heart. He would wait for the day he would hear it, but until then, he would make every effort possible to love his father unconditionally.

It was at this point in Billy's life that he learned what the word *compassion* really means in practice. He began to act out his Granny's example. At long last, he was able to see Cecil as a man who just needed Jesus. He made himself push aside his expectations of Cecil's being like Charles Ingles, the father from "Little House on the Prairie." To Billy, Cecil became a hurting sinner who needed a relationship with God. Regardless of how difficult it was to say, "I love you," Billy became determined to let Cecil know he truly did love him.

Billy learned the miracle of forgiveness and realized what Christ has to do in order to forgive us when we fail Him miserably. Never again would Billy be able to genuinely hate anyone. He remained faithful at church, and he worked in children's church with the music and puppet team. He and Jeff Sturgill, the pastor's son, became good friends. Billy worked with the bus ministry and visitation program as well. He became a leader at church and school and a father figure for his younger brothers. Despite an extreme amount of pressure, he embraced it with the strength he found in Christ, knowing that God was working all things together for the good of those that love the Lord, and Billy openly loved the Lord.

- *Chapter 10* -

Creating Character

During Billy's junior year of high school, he received his driver's license. It was a step toward the freedom he had always fantasized about, yet he knew that freedom, in the way he had dreamed, would never come. Childhood images of being part of a different family were now fading into the foggy past along with other memories that would best stay there for now. Billy was caught up in school activities and found a passion in succeeding at everything he attempted. He continued to stay involved in his high school band, while pursuing the arts, including drama.

Billy Wayne didn't fit the mold of a southwestern Virginia hillbilly teenager. Gate City High School in the late seventies and early eighties was renowned for its outstanding football teams and athletic prowess, as each year the school ranked highly in the state football playoffs. Billy knew that he wasn't like the other boys as far as athletic abilities, but he had always been outspoken and was not apologetic about who he was. Usually, boys that didn't fit the mold of being athletic lived quietly in the shadows, avoiding comments made by other students concerning their lack of athletic ability. Billy had spent too many years questioning God about his difference. Why didn't he like hunting and fishing? Why didn't he have a hunger to play sports? Only God knew of the attempts Billy had made to be passionate for the things that were acceptable in the eyes of other people, especially his dad. He would hear comments made behind his back at school suggesting that he was gay. Other times, fellow students were downright mean, taunting Billy about his size. Such remarks would momentarily immobilize Billy's confidence, but as he continually learned to draw strength from God about who he was, he found consolation in being pleasant to even those people he knew had made comments.

> "But I say to you, Love your enemies, bless them that curse you, do good to them that hate you, and pray for them which despitefully use you, and persecute you." Matthew 5:44 NIV

Most of his fellow students thought well of Billy, however, though no one knew the misery of his home life. He hid it well. Many teachers and school personnel saw the potential Billy possessed and helped him along the way.

Mrs. Gladell Crum, Billy's guidance counselor all throughout high school, had taken a special interest in him. He confided in her secrets he had never shared with anyone else. As she came to know Billy, she grew to love him and his zeal for life and the arts. She was often amazed at his talent and personality. Being a guidance counselor for several years, and working with many students, she recognized the inimitable qualities that radiated from Billy's life. Knowing much about his background, she was delighted that Billy chose to hang out with the good crowd at school. She recognized how eager he was to make people happy and observed how he used his talents to do so. Encouraging him was easy for her. Mrs. Crum often advised Billy on life matters, and he trusted her instruction.

She watched as Billy performed in the school's production of *The Wizard of Oz*, under the direction of Charles Phillips. His determination not just to perform, but to perform exceptionally well, made Mrs. Crum even more determined to encourage him in his talents. He could not only act, but he was a skilled artist as well. He also had an art teacher, Sharon Miller, who encouraged him to develop his artistic talents.

Mrs. Crum worried about Billy's physical well-being, as she observed his perseverance to succeed. His thin, frail body caused her to be gravely concerned. Often, she would ask Billy why he wasn't eating lunch. He would reply to her that he just wasn't hungry, but Mrs. Crum knew better. She was intuitive enough to know that either Billy had no money to buy lunch, or he was saving his money for something he needed. Because of their financial difficulties and the number of children in Billy's family, the Arrington's qualified for free lunches. Billy was ashamed to stand in line to have his free lunch ticket punched, so he would go without unless he had the money to purchase his own. Being sensitive to Billy's pride, Mrs. Crum would come up with clever methods to get him to eat—sometimes finding an extra lunch ticket lying around or asking Billy to go and pick up her lunch tray, then deciding she wasn't hungry after all and offering it to him. Her plots were always transparent to Billy, but they confirmed her care and concern, which only strengthened the bond of trust between them. Through her concern, she taught Billy to be a gracious receiver.

During this same time, Charles Phillips, Billy's theater and English teacher, encouraged Billy to think outside the box of Scott County, Virginia. He encouraged Billy to get involved in the Kingsport Theatre Guild. Billy played the villain lead in *The Odyssey of Jeremy Jack,* and later he went on to perform in *You're a Good Man, Charlie Brown,* which won him the Johnson Hilliard Cup, the guild's highest honor, for best actor. Billy also became more involved with 4-H and had the opportunity to perform in the Share-the-Fun talent show, and he won first place with a jazz dance to Frank Sinatra's "New York, New York." After that, he went on to win the regional and state competitions, despite the fact that he had never received any formal dance training. Through the experience, he was asked to travel and represent 4-H clubs, entertaining for different venues throughout the state of Virginia.

Seeing this talent emerge, Mrs. Crum sought to expose Billy to as much culture as possible, knowing that he would soak in everything he saw and heard, process it, and become a stronger person because of it. She scheduled visits to several colleges and created opportunities for him to be involved in state programs. During Billy's junior year of high school, he qualified to go on a trip for underprivileged teens to Richmond and Williamsburg, Virginia. Mrs. Crum would serve as a chaperone on the trip as well. She knew that Billy had never experienced a full social life of dating and became concerned when she saw him holding hands with a girl on the trip. Worried that it would be a turning point for Billy and that he might compromise his strong Christian beliefs, she prayed for him to be able to stay chaste and hold to his convictions. Her prayers were answered. Even then, Billy's convictions to stay pure began to take hold in his heart. He had always been honest with Mrs. Crum and had earlier confided to her his wish to remain pure.

Mrs. Crum cared about Billy, and he, in turn, not only cared about her but had great respect for her. She helped shape and nurture his young life and helped him be all he could be.

Mrs. Crum and her husband, Dewey, would often discuss Billy's life at length. Billy had shared some of his most hurtful experiences with her. He told her of his dad's affair, and of his naming the son from that affair Billy Jr.

It made him feel less special to Cecil than he already did. Billy also told Mrs. Crum about situations that were happening at home and the responsibilities that seemed to overwhelm him at times. Mrs. Crum's heart ached for Billy Wayne. She became one of his greatest supporters in life. It seemed she always saw greatness in him, and she once prophetically told Billy that she thought he would be a minister some day. He thought she must be crazy. All he knew about preachers were that they were mostly legalistic, wore three-piece polyester suits, and condemned the world to Hell. He could not imagine himself ever fitting that mold.

As Billy Wayne's senior year began in August of 1980, he searched out and visited several colleges. He anticipated the day that he could break free and escape all that held him down so he could start his own life. He felt like he had already raised a family. Soon, it would be time to go and fulfill all the plans that God had laid out for his life.

Becoming drum captain and alternate drum major gave Billy several opportunities to lead the band at ballgames and pep rallies during his last year of high school. He performed in theatre productions at Gate City High and also for Kingsport Theatre Guild, which won him the highest awards and trophies for his performances.

He had become an accomplished mime performer and continued with his ventriloquism. He won many awards for acting, writing, public speaking, and art, and he strived all the more to be successful. He immersed himself into activities that could be done in and around school hours.

Billy was determined to overcome his situation at home and was persistent to give God the glory for all of it. In any and all competitions, he always gave the glory to Christ. He knew he was nothing without Jesus; but with Jesus, the sky was the limit.

In January of Billy's senior year, his grandfather, Clyde Salling, died. This situation ultimately provided an escape for Billy Wayne. Because Mary Belle was left alone, Bethel allowed Billy to go back to the mountains, near Ft. Blackmore, and stay with her during the spring months. These unusual circumstances caused Billy and his granny's bond to grow stronger than ever. The Lord was also using this situation to help wean Billy from the care of his brothers. With Billy Wayne absent, Bethel had to resume the responsibilities that she had once carried as a mother. She had sown her wild oats and came to realize that her children were the most important things in her life. Now she would begin a journey that would lead her in a different direction altogether.

Billy had gained some popularity at school over the past four years, but it wasn't because of compromise or hanging with the in crowd. Billy never had time for that. People didn't always like Billy. He was a bold witness for Christ, and being a Christian had already proved expensive, as it had cost Billy his family at times. Being a Christian wasn't just a label to Billy. It carried with it a huge responsibility to be accountable for his actions. It was no different at school. He was conservative, opinionated, and truthful. People wanted to be around him because he stood for what was right. He never played favorites with social classes or race. He sought to be a young man of dignity and character; he strived not to care what others thought of him. If there were a challenge anywhere, he would take it. The storms of life continued to inspire him. They became an opportunity for him to jump into the midst of the tempest and scream to the whole world, "With God on my side, I will not run from anyone anymore!" In his small, wispy frame, there was a determination that would not back down. He was in competition with himself and his past. People saw that in him. When students would make fun of him, he disregarded the urge to vindicate himself. The opinions of others didn't matter. He sought the audience of one: Jesus Christ. He gave his best for God, because Billy knew God had given His best for him.

Eventually, Billy's high academic performance at Gate City earned him good standing to choose from several colleges that had accepted him. In February, Billy was accepted to Berea College in Berea, Kentucky. He knew that his time at home would be short and that this was his ticket to freedom and an opportunity to prove to the world that he was somebody.

In May of his senior year, the faculty selected Billy Wayne as Mr. Gate City High School. This award was given to the student that showed academic excellence and leadership. This was the first time in the history of Gate City High School that the honor had been given to a non-athlete. At the same time, the student body voted Billy as "Most Talented," but he was asked by the faculty to yield that title to someone else after he received the title of Mr. Gate City High School. Billy yielded the position, being thankful for the affirmation from the student body.

In June of 1981, Billy graduated Gate City High School as an honor student and in the top twenty in his class. He was also the president of National Honor Society. Be that as it may, the secrets and hidden abuse of his family was never disclosed. Aside from Mrs. Crum and a handful of Billy's closest friends, no one knew the obstacles that Billy had to overcome through the years just to walk across the stage and receive his diploma—a diploma that would free him from the life he was leaving behind, while it also enslaved him to the memories he was trying to escape."

- *Chapter 11* -

College Bound

In late August of 1981, Billy Wayne packed his belongings and headed off to Berea, Kentucky, to attend Berea College. Like most eighteen-year-olds, he was elated at the thought of living on his own. Cecil, Bethel, and Larry all went along for the trip. It was an exciting time for the entire Arrington family because Billy Wayne was the first to ever attend college.

They traveled to Berea a day earlier than Billy was to move into his dorm room, and therefore they got a room for the night at the Ramada Inn. A time that should have been a good memory turned dreadful that night. As usual, Cecil and Bethel got into an argument. Cecil got drunk and left the motel. Billy held in his frustrations at their typical behavior. He could not wait until the next morning to finally be freed from it all. The little room in Blue Ridge Dormitory would soon become his sanctuary away from all the fights, drunkenness, and general chaos that had been the custom up to this point in his life.

The next morning, Bethel, Cecil, and Larry acted as though nothing had happened. Billy had been appalled at their behavior the night before, and now he felt mere disgust that they would think it such a normal thing as not even to mention it. The trio helped Billy unload his belongings into his dorm room, and then they departed for the three-and-a-half-hour trip back home. After they left, Billy's emotions ran deeper than he could have ever expected. He felt sadness like he never imagined he would, yet a sense of freedom swept over him that balanced out all of his fears and anxieties. As he watched the taillights of the car disappear down the street and around the corner, his mind flashed a brief memory of the night before. Billy breathed a heavy sigh and returned to his room to unpack all of his familiar stuff. If this were going to be his world now, he would have to get settled in as quickly as possible.

Any apprehension about being separated from his family quickly vanished. The possibilities of becoming whatever he wanted to be were racing through his mind as he unloaded his belongings and arranged them around the room. No one here knew that his father had told him he wouldn't amount to anything. He didn't want anyone here to know about the past, at least not yet. He wanted people to love him for the person he was without associating him with his family secrets. All the baggage of his childhood and teen years was left back home, deep in the Appalachian Mountains of Virginia. He would not bring it here with him. It was much too heavy to carry around, and as far as he was concerned, it could stay buried as long as he didn't have to think about it any more. His past was one thing that he definitely would never miss.

After a couple hours of unpacking and settling into his room, Billy stood back to observe the new world he had just created for himself. Examining every inch of the room in detail, as was his nature, his eyes fixed upon the two Bibles that lay on top of his storage barrel.

Immediately after graduating Gate City High School, Billy knew that a major transformation was on the horizon. He knew that God was fanning the flame of a new work in his heart. Billy began to pray that God would give him a desire to read the Bible. He memorized a verse of Scripture every week. His prayer life and church attendance was perfect. Even though he had been a Christian for six years, Billy's Bible study habits were hit and miss. Billy had been given a paperback Bible from Tabernacle Baptist Church when he gave his life to Christ. But he wanted a real study Bible. He wanted to become a man of the Word.

God granted that request. Graduation Sunday came, and Billy was called to come to the front of the church along with other graduating seniors. The church presented Billy with a real leatherback Schofield Study Bible. As Billy was leaving the parking lot after the service, Lowell Lawson, a children's church worker, approached Billy. He was hesitant but handed Billy another Bible. It was a new Open Study Bible. Lowell said that God had laid it on his heart to give Billy this particular Bible. Billy took the Bible and thanked God for answering his prayer. God was driving Billy to a better understanding of Christianity and His Word. Billy knew that this was a sign from God to become a student of the Bible.

He walked over to the Bibles and lovingly picked them up. After musing over them momentarily, a thought that seemed to speak in a still, small voice revealed an earth-shattering truth to his soul, telling him that all the freedom he had ever desired was written upon the pages inside. Billy was hungry for knowledge and needed answers in his life that he knew only God had. Up until this point, he had relied heavily on the folks at Tabernacle Baptist Church to give him instruction concerning God's Word. Without the comfort of his home church and all of their guidance, Billy became aware that day of his awesome responsibility to be accountable to God. As he held his Bibles to his chest with a new sense of reverence, he humbly prayed and made a dedication to God to study His Word daily. That day literally changed his life forever, because Billy not only became a student of Berea College, but more importantly he became an apprentice of the Word of God. The very basic fiber that would be used to spin the tapestries of his life was supplied to him that day. The intimacy and comfort he found in the pages of his Bible transformed his life forever. God had begun building a foundation in him for a greater purpose than he ever could have imagined with this one commitment.

On Friday, September 4, 1981, Billy began his classes at Berea College. His schedule consisted of issues and values, man and the arts, math, stagecraft, play directing, and physical education. He was most looking forward to his issues and values class, as he had always enjoyed expressing his opinions and thoughts about various subjects.

On the next day, Saturday, Billy learned about the job he would have for the first semester. He would become a tour guide at the Appalachian Museum, which promoted the study and preservation of the Appalachian culture.

Billy's alarm clock didn't go off on Sunday morning, and he got up a little late. He still made it in time for breakfast and to catch the 9:25 a.m. church van that took him to Silver Creek Baptist Church. He had lived in Berea only a few days, but he knew he wanted to find a local church to attend. The service at Silver Creek Baptist was enjoyable, but it was quite different from what Billy was used to back home.

Billy was able to keep busy the first few weeks of college, and he loved learning new things. After about a month, when things began to slow down, his thoughts turned to his family, and he wondered how they were doing. Every day he would run to the post office and look in his little box. Sometimes he could see a small piece of paper in there, and he would excitedly run through the combination to retrieve the surprise waiting inside. Expecting a letter from someone back home, he was often forlorn to find the paper was only a flyer or junk mail to be distributed in the nearest waste basket. Other students often shrieked with delight when they received a letter from home. Billy was glad for them, but at the same time he would breathe a heavy sigh; he felt lonely. At that point, he had written nineteen letters home and had received only one from his mother.

As much as he hated some of the memories he had of home, Billy found himself more homesick than he expected to be. He worried that Bethel wasn't taking care of his brothers the way she should. Not hearing any news from home caused him to imagine the worst. Going away to college had seemed as though it would bring so much freedom, but now, Billy was realizing that it also brought an uneasiness that he had not anticipated. He wasn't home to take care of the situations any more, and he wondered if his family would be okay.

Though worried and concerned about life back home, Billy also knew that he wanted to excel in college. He would just have to give his worries to God and concentrate on where he was and what he was doing.

The longer Billy was at Berea College, the more involved he became with the activities there. He joined the Berea Country Dancers, and shortly afterwards, he tried out for a part in a one-act play called *Fancy Free* and got it. Three of his friends also received parts in the play. The next day, Billy received a phone call from Paul Power, professor of the drama department, who wanted Billy to begin practice for an opening show. Billy's talents were quickly becoming recognizable. He was the only freshman in his play-directing class, but his advisor, acknowledging his talents early, wanted him to be in there.

Billy also kept trying to find a church where he felt comfortable. More than anything, he missed his home church, Tabernacle Baptist, back in Kingsport. He would keep searching.

Eventually, family and friends started writing Billy more letters, and he began to feel connected with home again. He didn't have the opportunity to visit home often, but he looked forward to the times when he could. While preparing for his first weekend home, he had hoped that things there would be different. They were not. There was always some sort of a fuss going on. It grieved him each time he returned home. He missed his brothers and he knew they missed him too, but he was always glad to return to college.

After a few weeks in Berea, Billy began to see some of the changes that had taken place in him since he left home. He felt a sense of freedom from the responsibilities at home, and along with that freedom, he also experienced guilt. For the first time in his life, his decisions were centered on himself. His goals were about who and what he was. He didn't have to play a game of survival. In all his decisions, he was the only person he ever had to consider now. It was a freedom that he had never known.

Numerous activities, homework, and just hanging out with new friends occupied most of Billy's time now. He met many new people with so many different backgrounds. Acknowledging that each person needed Jesus the same sent him on a quest to find the truth. He began to question many of the legalistic views that he had learned growing up. Many questions ran through his mind: *Would long hair send you to Hell or was it the fact of not knowing Jesus Christ as your personal Savior the reason people went to Hell?* Although his home church back in Tennessee had been very strict in their legalistic views, Billy quickly learned that many of those viewpoints were failing the test. The confusion he felt from being at Tabernacle all those years and being taught doctrine that now puzzled him, such as not to allow your hair to touch your ears or collar, or "It's a sin for girls to wear pants, because that is men's clothing," or "Rock music is from the devil," or "Dancing is a sin," or "If a man has a full beard, it is a mockery of God," or "If you miss church, you aren't right with God," or "King James 1611 is the only true Word of God … any other version of the Bible is from Hell." Billy wanted the truth for himself. He loved the people at Tabernacle Baptist and realized they had helped to instill in him great truths about God, but he also knew the legalism he had been taught was not the truth.

One of the first friends Billy made at college was Chrissy Davis. She was a senior during Billy's freshman year. He was awestruck after hearing her haunting, folk-style voice singing a Christian song at a bonfire one night. There seemed to be an anointing on her that could have only come from God, and her countenance shone as one filled with the joy of the Lord. Billy knew there would be a lasting friendship between them. He had been praying for God to help him develop his gifts and talents. Chrissy took an interest in Billy and encouraged his singing. She told him he sang well. Chrissy wanted Billy to meet her at the music building a few days a week so they could sing Christian music together. He had already decided to take singing lessons, so this would be fun. Billy found it easy to sing harmony with Chrissy. Growing up in the mountains with family members who sang, he thought everyone could sing harmony easily. Chrissy was very encouraged at his talent and asked him to sing with her in chapel one Sunday evening. Billy was very nervous, as this was all new to him. He sang a duet with her of a song called "Spirit Song." Unbeknownst to Billy, Chrissy had invited members of the New Life Singers, a group to which she belonged, to this service. Afterwards, they asked Billy to be a part of their evangelistic singing group. He immediately agreed and was excited to get started. This was the beginning of the journey that led Billy Wayne down the road to becoming a contemporary Christian music artist.

Chrissy introduced Billy to Ms. Amboise-Chaumont, known to her students as Ms. A. C. She would be his voice instructor for the next four years. Ms. A. C. began teaching Billy on the level he was at musically. She knew he had no desire to become an opera star, yet he wanted to go into musical theatre. She trained him for that field. Even though he wouldn't be singing opera, she still held him to the strictest of disciplines with his voice training. Billy never had much confidence in his voice, even though he thoroughly enjoyed singing. After hearing Billy sing, Ms. A. C. allowed him to go into private voice classes. She began training his voice for stamina and power. Oftentimes, he stood in front of her piano and cried as she relentlessly taught him placement, tone, and support. Before singing lessons with Ms. A. C., Billy could only sing two songs before his voice was hoarse. Now he could sing for two hours. Ms. A. C. would snap, "Again, again, again ..." She never gave up. When Billy couldn't find his placement, she would try something else. He dreaded his vocal juries at the end of each semester, when he had to stand before the professors in the music department and be scrutinized at something that he felt he couldn't do very well. He often pretended that he was an opera singer and faked a confidence as he walked on the bare stage with nothing but a piano. Having to sing Italian, French, German, and Spanish made Billy feel empathy for those who had to listen to him. His evaluations would come back repeatedly telling him "Don't slide your notes," "Lift the tones," "Don't do glottal attacks," "Watch your pitch." In breaking the rules, he learned them. He became very grateful for Ms. A. C. and all of her patience and her disciplines as she taught him the world of voice training.

Professor Paul Power, the head director of the drama department, became one of the greatest supporters Billy had ever known. Paul saw something in Billy that led him to say that Billy was one of only two students he ever had that could make it in professional theatre. Paul and his wife, Barbara, both saw something special in Billy Wayne as they opened their home to him, and he became like a member of their family. They both loved him, and he loved them back. Paul was very practical in his approach to theatre. He had performed with Danny Kaye and other old movie stars and started a theatre during World War II in Germany. All of the U.S.O. performers would come and perform there. He had been the director of Kentucky's Outdoor Drama, *Wilderness Road*. Paul had also worked with Ned Beatty and had done television programs. He was truly a seasoned director, a performer, and most of all, a wonderful teacher.

Billy's life was being enriched with so many wonderfully talented and giving people. He was like a dry sponge, waiting to soak in the next lesson.

Through the drama department, Billy met many people. Each of those enjoyable friendships impacted his life. Mary Ann Shupe, who was the costumer at Berea College, worked closely with Billy during the production of *Billy Bishop Goes to War*, *The Lark*, and *Aladdin*. They developed a great friendship, and Billy learned a lot from her insights into costuming.

Billy also met Steve Griffith his freshman year. Steve was a sophomore and lived a couple of doors down from Billy and his roommate, Rob Hines. Rob was Catholic, and Billy learned much about the Catholic faith from him. Steve was a baseball jock who seemed to have all the girls, and Billy was a theatre major. Their paths seldom crossed, but when they did, Steve was very compassionate with Billy and always tried to encourage him. Steve didn't tolerate anyone harassing his new friend. Billy's junior year landed him in another dormitory, Edwards Building. Steve was already living there and had arranged, behind Billy's back, for him to be transferred to his dorm. Through a lottery for single rooms, Billy ended up there. At first, Billy didn't want to be there, but the idea grew on him.

It was that year that Billy directed a dance production that was a revue of past musicals. He held auditions, and Steve Griffith showed up. The challenge for the production was to take non-dancers and transform them into stage performers. Billy needed athletic guys that could lift the girls, and Steve was a natural for the part. The show was a success. Some of Steve's baseball friends were part of the show as well. That is when baseball met theatre, and Berea College was forever changed.

Steve and Billy's friendship grew closer, and they began hanging out together. Steve's room was just down the hall from Billy's. They would invite girls over to their rooms and cook for them. Billy and Steve served them spaghetti out of a Purina dog bowl with plastic forks.

Steve loved the girls in college, and he liked to party as well as anyone. Billy was constantly and consistently up in his face over these issues, because he knew Steve wasn't where he should be spiritually. Steve wanted Billy around him only when he was feeling spiritual or going through a crisis. Billy grew tired of Steve's ups and downs and found himself in a love/hate relationship with him. He often questioned God as to why He had allowed Steve to be part of his life. Steve exhausted Billy with his inconsistencies, yet Billy couldn't let go of their friendship. Billy grew all the more impatient; but he wasn't aware at the time that Steve was watching his life, and they too would become lifelong friends as God would eventually place a call on Steve's life to go into the ministry.

Billy made another friend his freshman year, a girl by the name of Kamini Desi from Bangladesh. She was Hindu, but she was open to listening to Billy's Christian views and showed a genuine respect toward Billy for what he believed. Once again, God was teaching Billy how big and vast His world was.

Billy's freshman year was as much of a culture shock as anyone could have experienced. Not only was God teaching him to minister to people outside the legalistic boundaries he had been taught, but he was seeing a side of life that he had never before seen. Billy was exposed to openly gay people for the first time in his life. It made him angry that anyone would live in such opposition to the Scriptures. Through prayer, he learned to "hate the sin, yet love the sinner." Upon taking his first job at the Appalachian Museum, he was hit on by a belligerent, openly gay supervisor. The supervisor taunted Billy by calling him "Jerry Falwell" and told him he needed to be more accepting of other people.

One day, Billy was called into the Dean of Students' office. Co-workers who were sympathetic to Billy's predicament reported that the supervisor had been harassing Billy at work. The supervisor was then put on probation by the college. God had vindicated Billy. After realizing Billy wasn't going to retaliate or show hatred toward him for the way he had treated him, the supervisor became very apologetic. A year after this incident, the supervisor came to Billy and expressed how much he respected him and his stand for Christ. Billy learned what compassion meant. God was stretching Billy's boundaries and helping him understand that people needed Christ regardless of their race, sexual orientation, or religion.

The last three years at Berea would mark a major turning point in Billy's life. He had planned his future and would work and study hard to become what he had always wanted to be. After years of watching the Academy Awards and Grammy Awards on television, with tears welling up in his eyes, and declaring that one day he would be on that stage receiving an award, signifying he had made it, his goal was in sight. That goal raised him high above the world he lived in daily. It was a dream that gave Billy Wayne Arrington the drive to *be* somebody.

Shawn, Seth and Bobbi Jo Bennett

Maudie Arrington's Home, Speers Ferry, VA

Maudie and Enoch Arrington

Bethel & Cecil as teens just before marriage

Billy & Donna in foreground. Cecil & Larry carrying Shannon & Gerald

Mary Belle & Clyde Salling Home, Ft. Blackmore, VA

Mary Belle & Clyde Salling

Donna, Billy & Randy Fishing in the Holston River

Wood Riverview Baptist Church, Wood, VA

Billy Wayne, Crowned King at Weber City Elementary

Bobby & Ruth Hensley in the 70's

Bethel & Cecil Arrington (early 70's)

Gerald, Shannon, Donna, Billy & Randy 1979

Billy Wayne's Home growing up

Gate City High Band Captains (Billy — bottom right) 1981

Billy Wayne (Berea College Repertory Theatre)

New Life Singers (Berea College 1981-1985)

College Graduation 1985 (Cecil, Billy & Bethel)

Billy & Chrissy Davis at Smoky Mtn. Passion Play

Billy & cast members of Annie at Nashville Playhouse

Brock & Arrington Blended Family 1994

Billy & Mary Belle at her home

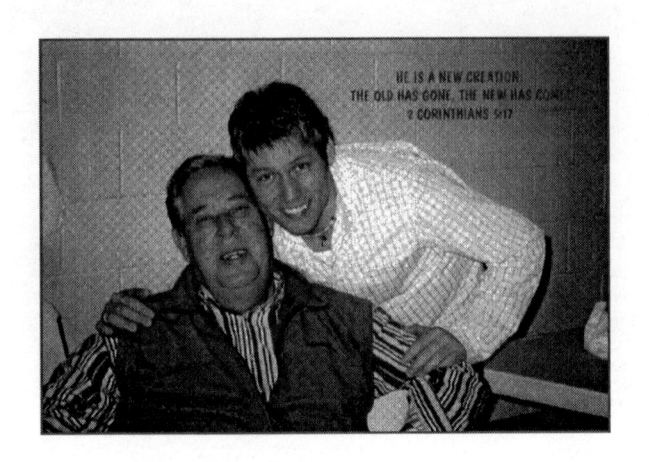

Billy Wayne & Cecil 2007

Steve & Jenny Griffith with Sarah, Chloe & Stephen

LampLight Theatre in Fall 2010

Billy with the cast of Journey's End at LampLight

Billy and Josh Reedy (DecembeRadio) at Dove Awards

Billy Wayne & Kimberly Holbrook

Billy, Sam Davis & Ridgemond Anthony Mosley

Billy Wayne Arrington 2011

- *Chapter 12* -

You Win, God.

"We're going to see *our* names on those lights someday, Billy," Vicki stated matter-of-factly, with stardust twinkling in her eyes as they walked away from Radio City Music Hall.

Billy Wayne and Vicki Hayes had become acting buddies. They both started out at Berea College the same year in theatre and became friends in their private lives as well as on stage. Billy won the respect of Vicki's parents, Effie and Glen, and when he wasn't singing with New Life in concert, he attended church with them. They treated him like a son. Billy often worried that Vicki did not place as much trust in Christ as she should have. She struggled with her faith daily and never seemed to develop a real personal relationship with Christ. Vicki admired Billy's faith and was very supportive of him in his walk with the Lord. He thought of her as a sister, as he often found himself worrying about her and wanting the best for her life. She confided in Billy about the guys she dated, and he gave her brotherly advice as she trusted his counsel.

Billy and Vicki aspired to go to New York as they excelled in the theatre program at Berea College. They were both selected to apprentice with the Berea College Summer Repertory Theatre. Both held offices for the Berea Players Theatre Group and Alpha Psi Omega, a theatre honorary. Their names were well known around the campus theatre circle for excellence in acting.

During the summer between their junior and senior year, Billy and Vicki went to New York City and stayed with Roy Steinberg, who had served as an artist in residence at Berea College and was a mentor for both of them. Vicki's mom agreed to let her go, knowing that Billy would be looking out for her best interest. They stayed with Roy and attended several productions on Broadway, Radio City Music Hall, Off-Broadway, and Off-Off Broadway. They were able to get a genuine feel for the whole city aspect of living as actors in New York City. Excited about being in New York and being exposed to the many theatre genres, Billy and Vicki made an agreement that when they graduated, they would move to New York to live and find work. Billy was not yet fully aware of what it would cost him to serve Christ.

Upon returning to Berea that summer and starting classes in the fall, Billy began working with Marlena Lustik, the new artist in residence at Berea College. Marlena was a professional director from New York and brought with her a wealth of experience in dance and humor. She directed Billy Wayne in the one-man, full-length musical comedy production of *Billy Bishop Goes to War*, in which Billy Wayne played the lead character, a World War I flying ace, as well as a host of friends and enemies, seventeen characters in all. The role demanded an actor who could sing, dance, and play a multiplicity of roles; it was the best and most difficult role of his student career. The lines he had to learn for the production would have been a challenge for even a seasoned actor, but Billy Wayne did a tremendous job. The three nightly performances of *Billy Bishop Goes to War*, performed at the Ross Jelkyl Drama Center, opened to a full house and ended with a standing ovation. Local newspapers reported that the play was a huge success. The flood of cards, letters, and flowers from friends, teachers, and well-wishers overjoyed Billy and gave him a sense of satisfaction that he had worked hard and given so many people an enjoyable performance.

Marlena wrote Billy Wayne a note to encourage him before he went on stage for the production:

> *Dear Billy,*
>
> *You are just wonderful in this play! Thank you for making* Billy Bishop Goes to War *everything I had hoped it would be.*
>
> *It's been a great pleasure working with you. You are quite an outstanding talent and now it's your show. You* are *Billy Bishop!*
>
> *Time to "fly."*
>
> *Love, Marlena*

Later in the term, he and Marlena had the opportunity to act together in a production of *Can You See Me Yet?*

Marlena continued to encourage Billy Wayne in his acting career through cards and letters after she returned to New York. She saw a tremendous talent in Billy that made her stretch out her arms to help him along.

During Billy's senior year at Berea, Paul Power had made plans to leave the college, but he wanted to stay until Billy graduated. Dr. John Bolin would be Paul's replacement. The two men approached theatre from different angles. Billy had learned under Paul's practical, hands-on approach for the last three years. Dr. Bolin took more of an academic approach to theatre. He taught his students about modern approaches through experimental theatre, and at the same time, he encouraged them to learn all about theatre history. He was an extremely intellectual professor. Both Dr. Bolin and Paul Power were strict when it came to instructing their students. Dr. Bolin didn't hand out compliments easily.

Paul Power loved new faces and new talent and was willing to take risks when no one else would. He had a gift for seeing everyone's potential. He had helped Billy to design his independent major in music/theatre. Paul took Billy under his wing and truly became a mentor. He went before the academic committees on Billy's behalf. When Billy was at Berea, the only theatre majors available were to those who declared independent majors. Billy had to write up a proposal and it had to be approved by Berea's board of directors. Then it had to cross three different departments in order for him to secure his major. Paul intervened for Billy until the process was completed and approved.

Paul opened doors for Billy to direct shows unlike those ever done before. During Billy's senior year, Billy was asked by the campus activities director to direct a dinner theatre for the college.

Dr. Bolin was furious at the thought of doing theatre out of the proper setting, and he did not want Billy to do it. Theatre productions should be done in the theatre! It would be a conflict of interest. Under no circumstances was Billy to do it!

Paul Power had been in Massachusetts working on some playwriting. He came back to the college and fought the battle for Billy. He felt that it was important for Billy to have the opportunity to direct the dinner theatre. This caused a major conflict between the two professors, and there was much tension. Paul knew the theatre department did not have the proper facilities to host a dinner theatre, but he felt it was an honor for Billy to be asked by the campus activities department. At that point, Billy had performed in over forty productions at Berea, acted as assistant director for several productions in the community, and had been the director of six productions associated with Berea College. He had already earned every acting, directing, and technical award of the theatre department.

Regardless of Billy's capabilities, Dr. Bolin wasn't happy with Paul or Billy. Billy felt as though Dr. Bolin gave him the cold shoulder for the next four months.

Billy went ahead with the dinner theatre during January of his last semester. He directed *You're a Good Man, Charlie Brown*. Every performance was packed, and Billy was even able to earn college credits for directing the show. He also earned an award from the college for directing Berea College's first dinner theater.

The end of Billy's college career was drawing near. He had prepared well for theatre and was looking ahead to his future. Still singing with New Life Singers and sharing his testimony at concerts helped him to remain focused on the calling God had placed on his life.

Marlena Lustik was impressed with Billy's drive and ability. After working with him during his senior year, she showed a video of *Billy Bishop Goes to War* to Dustin Hoffman, the actor, producer, and director. Hoffman was impressed with Billy's performance and ability. He, along with Roy Steinberg, invited Billy Wayne to New York for auditions upon his graduation. Billy was thrilled. His dreams were coming true. He already had some of the industry's best telling him that he could make it and he knew he could.

Something deep inside of Billy Wayne began to question the direction he was going...

> *What is this stirring deep inside of my soul? This is what I have worked for my whole college career.*
>
> *What are you asking me, God?*
>
> *You know I will follow You, Lord, wherever You lead me. I would never compromise my love for You. Just show me, Lord. Show me what it is You are trying to tell me. Make it clear to me.*
>
> *My greatest desire is to please You, above everything else in my life, but I don't understand. I want to tell others of Your amazing saving grace and I thought this was the avenue You wanted me to go down.*

> *Every time I am on stage and I have an opportunity, I give You all the praise, God. I thought this is what You wanted from me.*
>
> *I don't understand.*

So much was happening in Billy Wayne's life. He had just been invited by Dustin Hoffman to come to New York and audition. Meanwhile, he had also become co-leader of the New Life Singers. There was a burning desire he could not explain that caused him to want to tell people about Christ. During the concerts he performed with New Life, he inevitably would end up sharing his faith with the audience. There was an urgency that gripped his heart heavily to tell people about what God had done in his life. He wanted to share the story about his Savior with the whole world.

In May of 1985, Billy found out that he was going to receive the highest award that could be given to a Berea graduate. The award would be announced at commencement and given to him by Alex Haley, author of *Roots*. Billy was stunned by the news. This particular award was decided on solely by the president of Berea College and was based on scholastic excellence and leadership. In the history of Berea College, no one in the arts program had ever received this award.

In contrast to the invitation to go to New York and audition, Billy also had an opportunity to go to Yellowstone National Park and work for a Christian ministry in the National Parks. His longtime friend, Chrissy Davis, had been working for them and offered Billy the opportunity to come to Yellowstone and share his faith.

God had placed a burning desire in Billy's heart. "God's will … it has to be done."

Billy felt as though he was being ripped in two.

Marlena was waiting on an answer from Billy. Pressure was building upon him. He had to make a decision, soon!

Billy sought the will of God in a deep prayer:

> *Lord, I will give You whatever You ask for, though I still don't understand. This is the one thing I was able to accomplish that I can earn a living at. Why are You asking me to give up something that means so much? Why did You let me waste the last four years of my life working so hard for something that You were going to require me to lay aside?*

So many people will be greatly disappointed with me. Paul Power poured so much into my life. Marlena is waiting on an answer from me. She went out of her way to get me this interview. I am receiving the highest award for all my work. What will everyone think? They will think I have gone mad to have worked so hard to achieve so much and walk away from it all.

God, this is so hard. This doesn't make sense in the real world.

I know I cannot carry the torch You handed to me and pursue my own dreams.

I cannot take this conflict within my soul any longer.

You win, God. I surrender!

Here it is, God. With this heavy, but willing heart, I lay before You every gift You have ever given me. Here are my talents, my goals, and my dreams of becoming an actor or director.

I have no idea where You are leading me, but I am willing. You are worthy of any of these sacrifices.

All I am and all I have, at this moment I give to You.

Billy felt flushed as he grieved the death of his dreams and at the same time celebrated in his spirit as a newfound freedom swept though his soul, with the Holy Spirit assuring him that his decision had been the right one. There was not even an ounce of doubt in his mind. He never looked back.

Billy knew his decision to align himself with a calling higher than Hollywood or New York would come at a great price. It became evident to him that God had been preparing him for ministry all of his life. Billy, who was already making a huge career change, also made a vow to never charge for the gospel message that God had given him to share with others. God would be his provider and his ever present help in times of trouble.

Billy's acting career ended as soon as it began, but God was watching.

- *Chapter 13* -

Long-Awaited Words

As Billy dedicated more of his time to Bible study and grew closer to God in his prayer life, he never lost the desire to see his parents come to serve God. Being away from home during his college years had dulled the pain that Billy felt where his parents were concerned. The pain had been replaced with a grave burden for both Cecil and Bethel's spiritual well-being. Billy understood that his parents could never change their bad habits unless they surrendered their lives to God. Cecil was still drinking alcohol excessively, and Bethel continued to party at the bars. Billy purposely initiated contact with them both. He loved his parents, but sometimes he wondered if he was still seeking approval from the one person he had failed to impress as a child. Even as an adult, he desired his father's attention and wanted more than anything to hear him say, "I love you, Billy, and I'm proud of you."

During Billy's last year of college, he began to perform more solos during the New Life concerts. He traveled back to his hometown to do a concert at Tabernacle Baptist. Billy saw his dad come in the church and sit far in the back. He was aware of where his dad was seated during the entire concert and prayed silent prayers that Cecil would come to know Jesus as his Lord and Savior that night. Billy and his friends from New Life went to the altar and prayed that Cecil would surrender his life to God. When he didn't, Billy was upset with God and questioned why God wouldn't save his dad that night.

When the evening was over and everyone was departing, Cecil came to Billy and asked him to call when he returned to college. Billy was puzzled, because even though there had been some progress in their relationship, they still weren't close enough to carry on a phone conversation.

Billy did as his dad had asked him. He arrived back at Berea College and walked to a campus pay phone to call Cecil. Trying to make conversation, he told his dad he had a safe trip. Billy became rather puzzled, as he could hear his father sobbing on the other end of the line. He could not recall Cecil's ever being in this state of mind, much less crying. Billy knew something was up, so he waited for his father to speak.

"Billy," Cecil sobbed, "I love you and I'm proud of you."

Those fragile yet empowering words, spoken through the handset of a pay phone, emphatically changed Billy Wayne that night. He would never again feel contempt for his dad. Something that had woven a black thread through the tapestry of his life was suddenly unraveling. He somehow felt stronger, empowered by the frailty of a few words spoken by the one man who had the influence to grant him immunity from the constant demon of disdain. Only healing remained. Billy knew now, more than ever, that he truly wanted to see Cecil find resolution in his own life. He would pray for his dad till the day he would see him saved. It would become a major part of his subsistence.

In deep thought, he walked back to his dorm room, fell on his knees, and wept uncontrollably at the thought of being loved by his father and making him proud. Through tears, he thanked God for the changes He was making in Cecil's heart. That day brought light to some of the darkest corners of Billy's soul as he began sorting through memories and resentments being held captive as witnesses of his contempt for Cecil. Billy knew he had to set the prisoners of his thought life free that day if he were ever to find freedom himself. God gave him the strength to do that. He no longer needed the bad memories of Cecil. He actually found himself wanting to get to know his dad and become part of his life.

- *Chapter 14* -

A New Mama

"Won't you come along and go with me?" Those were the only words Bethel could remember from the evening as she sat in the second row during the church service. The preacher had given a sermon, but Bethel couldn't remember a word he had said. Her spirit was talking to God, telling Him all of the things she had done wrong in her life. Though God already knew, Bethel knew she had to confess her sins to the Lord and let Him know that she knew what she had done wrong. Her three sisters and one brother-in-law had a quartet, and she had gone to hear them sing. It was the last song of the evening, and the words "Won't you come along and go with me?" resounded through her mind. She began to break apart on the inside. That is what she wanted more than anything … to go with God. Years of sin and denial were crumbling around her as the Spirit of God was penetrating her innermost being. She began to weep and cry out, "That is what I need! That is what I want!"

Bethel's feet were leading her outside the church that night after the services had ended, but her heart wouldn't allow her to go. She was headed down the steps on the outside of the church, but she made herself turn around and go back inside. Her sister, Beverly, talked with her as she poured her heart out to God. She asked Jesus to forgive her of all the wrongs in her life through brokenness and tears.

Immediately after Bethel's salvation, she told Beverly that she wanted to go see their mother. Bethel wanted to tell her the news, and she couldn't wait to call Billy Wayne, who was now working in Banner Elk, North

Carolina, at Lees-McRae College, and tell him. She did exactly that. She went to Mary Belle's house and told her that she had asked God's forgiveness and invited Jesus into her heart. Mary Belle began to shout with joy as they embraced each other. Bethel was thrilled to tell her mom, and then she asked Mary Belle if she could use her phone to call Billy Wayne. Mary Belle was more than happy to allow Bethel to use her phone.

In the spring of 1986, Billy had moved to Banner Elk to work at Lees-McRae College as a residence assistant (R.A.) and to help out in their performing arts department. Steve Griffith had moved to Banner Elk from Valdosta State University in Georgia to take the position of director of development. He wanted Billy to move there as well and had told him about the position of residence assistant. God had been working on Steve, but Steve was stubborn.

Billy remained consistent in sharing Christ with the students at the college. A great revival broke out on campus. Billy was pressed into acting as campus minister since the college had none at the time.

His position as R.A. landed him in the basement level of Avery Dormitory. Billy had a way with troubled students. They seemed to listen and trust him. Many students were placed on Billy's floor because of their behavioral, emotional, or academic struggles. Though persecuted for his convictions, the faculty and administration still had to recognize that Billy had an incredible rapport with hurting students. Billy's floor was soon referred to as the "last chance" floor. This was often the last stop before suspension from the college.

Billy had a great burden for the college. Even though it was a Christian college (with Presbyterian roots), they had no campus minister. Billy had no choice but to lead the students in their spiritual quest.

When Billy arrived at the college, the only active Christian group on campus was Fellowship of Christian Athletes. When he went to their first meeting, all they talked about was sponsoring a social. There were no Bible studies, discipleship, or accountability. Billy spoke up at the meeting and challenged them to go deeper. He offered to help sponsor and lead a Bible study once a week. He told them that in order to reach the campus for Christ, they would have to pray and ask God for revival.

That's exactly what happened. Revival came. More and more students were coming to know Christ and were hungry for Bible study. Lees-McRae, a.k.a. "Lead 'em Astray," was beginning to change. The students' hunger for the word instigated two additional Bible studies during the week. One was called "Happy Hour." It seemed to bring the curious partiers in to hear the truth. The football team wanted to start their own Bible study, which Billy led on Friday nights. The players were choosing God over partying.

Billy had met another R.A. that shared the same burden. His name was Randy Neff. God really used them together to spread the good news. Randy played the guitar and led in worship as Billy led in teaching. God was doing something beyond them that couldn't be contained on the campus.

Billy had a burden for the students to have a full-time campus minister and rallied with them to get a petition together to see it happen. He was getting physically tired of ministering and doing his job as an R.A. He went to Brad Crane, the president of the college, with the petition. Billy knew that Brad was a professing Christian; he told Brad that God would hold him responsible for the spiritual welfare of every student on the campus. Billy gave Brad suggestions on how to fund the salary and the housing for a ministry intern. Brad tried to be diplomatic, but when Billy laid down the petition with over 750 student signatures, he was speechless.

Brad finally agreed that something needed to be done. He suggested that Billy do the best he could in leading the students the rest of the semester. He promised to try to get someone in by fall semester.

This confrontation cost Billy. Billy's supervisor had to evaluate him in the coming weeks. She would tell him that his Christian witness was too strong. Billy asked her if she was a Christian. He knew that she professed to be. She replied positively, saying that she respected everything that Billy did. Billy proceeded to tell her the same thing that he told Brad Crane. He told her of her spiritual responsibilities to the students. He couldn't understand why a school would only use Jesus when it was convenient. He told them they were hiding behind a mask of Christianity and that they needed to be there spiritually for the students.

Billy's compassion for the students far outweighed his care for job security. He knew what was happening with the students. Every week, students were being saved, but there was no support from the administration.

Billy's supervisor had written on his evaluation: "Christian witness is too strong." After the conversation, she apologized and offered to remove the notation. Billy told her to leave it alone. He told her that it was the greatest compliment she could ever give him and when she got to heaven, she could explain that one to Jesus.

So, the move to Banner Elk was obviously not a smooth one. Billy's passion for Christ and ministry put a strain on his relationship with Steve, who worked in the administrative offices as director of development. Steve loved having Billy around, but Billy's presence brought conviction. Steve liked talking to Billy when he needed to ease his conscience of his disobedience in not following God's call. Billy loved Steve but wouldn't allow Steve's compromise to pull him down. Billy was praying that Steve would change. There was a large mission ahead of them in reaching the students at Lees-McRae.

After months of prayer, God allowed Billy to confront Steve. They went out to eat, and at the end of the evening, Billy took the liberty to express his burden. He told Steve that he loved him, but that he had absolutely no respect for him as a Christian. He cried as he said that Steve stood opposed to everything that God was trying to accomplish. Through his tears, Billy expressed compassion for Steve but intolerance for his lifestyle and behavior. He told Steve, "I have always been here for you. I have always tried to live Jesus in front of you. You have never been there for me as a brother in Christ. All you do is play games with God. I can't be around you anymore. All you do is pull me down. You say you love God, but you treat Him like dirt. Just because your dad is a preacher and the president of a seminary doesn't make you anything. You need to start standing in your own faith. I will be here for you, Steve. But until you make a change, I don't want you there for me. I don't trust you and I never will. I will never look up to you as a spiritual leader."

When Billy slammed the door to Steve's car, he thought that would be the end of a five-year friendship. Billy had seen a revival sweep across the campus and really needed God to send help to disciple the new believers. He was tired and felt alone.

Steve had to leave for a conference the next day. Needless to say, he had a lot to think about. About midweek, Billy was kneeling by his bed praying for God's direction in leading the Lees-McRae students. He was also feeling a heavy burden for his mother and knew that God was at work. He was weary and needed to hear from God.

Billy's phone rang. On the other end was a familiar voice, reading Scripture after Scripture. The words struck a chord in his heart. The truths ministered to his soul. It was Steve.

Steve told Billy that God had worn him out and that after Billy had confronted him, he went back to his apartment. God dealt with him pretty heavily. He told Billy that he had renewed His relationship with Christ and that God had changed him completely. Something was different this time. The Holy Spirit had used Steve to minister to Billy.

After Steve returned from his trip, he partnered with Billy and helped in the spiritual development of many of the students and faculty at the college. Steve had become a partner in ministry with Billy, and for the first time, they both felt the power of Christ at work in their relationship. They became soul mates and felt each other's burdens, including Billy's burden for his parents.

The last time Billy was home to visit, Bethel was again living with Larry Bledsoe. Billy was grieved over what she was doing and tried to talk to her about it. She knew he was right, but this was just the life she was accustomed to living. Billy left, feeling heavily burdened for his mom that weekend.

Billy found himself praying that if God had to take his life for his parents to come to know the Lord, then he was willing. When he told his mom what he had been praying, she became very upset with him and told him never to say that prayer again. Bethel knew how strong Billy was becoming in his faith, and it somehow made her afraid. She knew he was right; he had always been right in trying to get her to clean her life up, but now his prayers were weighing heavy on her heart. What if God did take Billy's life to get her attention? How could she ever live knowing that?

Bethel began to take account of her life. She felt as though she had gone too far to ever turn back to God. Billy kept telling her differently.

This particular night about 9:30, Billy received a call from Bethel. Her voice on the other end of the phone was somehow different from what he could ever remember. She almost shouted with elation as she greeted him, "Billy, you'll never guess where I went tonight!" He was clueless and urged her to tell him.

"I went to church, Billy! I went to church!"

He waited to hear more, now recognizing the joy in her voice.

"I knew I had to go to the service tonight. I even took off work to go," she added.

"And?" Billy probed her further.

"The service was over and I was walking down the steps outside the church to leave, but I just couldn't leave. I turned around and ran back to the preacher and told him that I needed to ask Jesus into my heart tonight!"

Billy was standing in his dorm apartment when he received the call. He could hear his granny in the background shouting, "Thank you Jesus! Glory hallelujah! Praise the Lord!"

Bethel continued, "Billy, I want to thank you for praying for me all these years and never giving up on me. Thank you for showing me Jesus!"

Billy longed to be there celebrating with her and his granny. He went and told Steve what was going on back home. Steve began to shout with Billy as they celebrated Bethel's salvation. Billy told all the guys in the dorm that had been praying for her. The good news spread across the campus.

Billy couldn't wait to get back home to see his mom. He gassed up his rickety old AMC Pacer that had a hole in the floor board and headed home to see her the next weekend. With $52 in his pocket, he wanted to buy his mom her own Bible with her name engraved on it. He stopped by the Moody Bible Bookstore in Kingsport, took a Bible to the counter, and the sales clerk rung it up on the register.

"That will be $51.50," the clerk said.

> *"But my God shall supply all your need according to his riches in glory by Christ Jesus." Philippians 4:19*

Billy didn't care that it was taking all his money to buy the Bible. He knew it would be the best investment he could ever make.

When he arrived at his mother's house, he kept the Bible hidden behind him as he knocked on the front door. Usually he would just go on in, but he wanted to surprise her. When she came to the door, Billy was the one who got the big surprise. He momentarily forgot about the Bible when he saw her face. There was such an astonishingly visible change over her whole demeanor. God had literally changed her, and it was as visible on the outside as it was on the inside. They grabbed one another in an embrace as they wept loudly with tears of joy. It was a day that Billy would never forget. God had truly answered his prayers and had given him a new mama.

Bethel had already kicked Larry out of her house. Billy was thankful that she was taking the initiative to straighten up her life. He was so afraid that Bethel wouldn't be strong enough to make all the changes, so he continued to pray for her daily.

After several months had passed, Bethel called Billy and told him she had been praying for God to place someone in her life to help her grow in her walk with the Lord. Billy had the same burden. He had been praying for someone to disciple her. Bethel told him about a man she had met at work. Billy couldn't help but think, *here we go again!*

Bethel insisted on telling Billy about the man. His name was Hubert Brock and he was a deacon in the First Assembly of God Church. His wife had died three years ago. Billy listened. Bethel continued telling him how Brock prayed with her every day on their lunch break. He gave her tapes of Christian music and sermons to listen to. Billy was skeptical about this man but wanted to meet him. He didn't sound like the kind of man that Bethel had been attracted to in the past.

Billy eventually met Brock and was awed by how God had placed such a wonderful Christian man in his mom's life. Bethel and Brock soon married, and Billy couldn't have been happier. He felt such gratitude for this man who was taking care of his mother and being the Christian influence and leader of their household.

- *Chapter 15* -

Dreamcoats and Repentant Thieves

Lees-McRae College opened Billy's eyes and heart for new avenues of ministry. In 1986, while at the college, Billy had the opportunity to participate in the performing arts program. Billy was asked by the director, Dr. Janet Carrol, to play the lead in *Joseph and the Amazing Technicolor Dreamcoat*. This was the first show that Billy had seen on Broadway in New York. It was always his desire to play this role before he was too old. Now, God had shown favor.

Billy thought of the time he had given theatre and his stage talents back to God. He wasn't certain that he would ever act again. Now, God was affirming him. Being the lead in a production wasn't Billy's drive anymore. He only wanted everyone to know who he was performing for. He wanted God to get the glory for his performances.

Joseph was one of Billy's favorite characters from the Bible. This production had all the elements of a Broadway show but carried a story and message from the Bible. Billy could identify with Joseph as an underdog who overcame overwhelming obstacles. Billy, like Joseph, had been treated as an outcast in his own family. Just as Joseph was imprisoned, so Billy had been spiritually growing up. God then exalted Joseph to second in command over a nation. Billy was beginning to realize the awesome position that God had placed him in both at Lees-McRae and in ministry.

The production of *Joseph and the Amazing Technicolor Dreamcoat* was a huge success. So much so, that the college would later contact Billy for an encore performance. The production was also entered into a national drama competition and would be critiqued by professionals from New

York. There was much anticipation the night the critic showed up to review the performance.

After viewing the production, the critic asked to have a private audience with Billy. He wanted to know why Billy was at this small college town and not in New York or working in a professional theatre company. He invited Billy to come to New York so that he could introduce him to some influential people in the professional theatre world.

Once again, Billy was faced with a big choice. This time his response was much quicker and more confident. Billy's response was simply, "This is where God has me now. I'm not certain why God has me here, but He is teaching me some things." As much as Billy wanted to take the critic's offer, he had no peace about it. It was a bittersweet moment for Billy. Once again, worldly success had knocked on Billy's door, and he chose the path that God was leading.

This encounter was also a charge of encouragement to Billy. He had often wondered if he was really good enough to play on Broadway. He needed to know that his skills were comparable to his contemporaries. This critic had answered those questions. The confirmation was clear, and Billy was assured that he had nothing to prove to the theatre world. He only wanted to remain faithful to the task that God had put before him.

The production of *Joseph* ... had opened Billy's eyes to even greater possibilities. It was here that Billy realized that musical theatre could be used as a tool to spread the message of God's word through entertainment. The Lord began to give Billy a greater vision of ministry and a unique sense of the use of his talents. All of the years of training and sacrifice began to make sense.

During summer break of 1986, Billy came back to Kingsport to work for the Boys Club. It was a rough summer. Billy was hired as the fine arts director. He supervised art classes, woodshop, crafts, and creative arts. He felt stifled by the overbearing director of the center. Billy's philosophy on working with troubled inner city children was quite different from that of his supervisor. They would go round and round on issues concerning the boys. Billy was easily frustrated with leaders who worked with children just for a paycheck. He wanted to invest in the lives of the children. And he did. Every opportunity he had, he shared his faith without apology. He wanted nothing more than to be an encouragement to those who felt trapped by their circumstances. He wanted to give them hope and a reason to live for their future. God was planting in Billy's heart discernment in recognizing the needs of high-risk students. Billy was developing a burden for inner city and underprivileged students.

Billy made it through the summer and found himself back at Lees-McRae College for the fall semester. Brad Crane brought on a new staff member to help with the spiritual needs of the students; she would act mainly as a campus activities director and assist with organizing Christian events. To Billy, it was nothing more than a compromise. He still continued to lead the Bible studies. Billy's faithful companion, Randy Neff, did not return to Lees-McRae due to burnout. However, Steve Griffith was by Billy's side helping with the Bible studies and Christian activities. Their friendship grew stronger than ever. Billy finally had in Steve what he had always longed for. God was doing a great work in both of their hearts. Neither of them knew how God would use them in ministry together over the next several years.

Steve's brother, Jimmy Griffith, moved to Banner Elk to spend his last year of high school with Steve. He and Billy became close during this time. Billy worked with Avery County High School that semester in choreographing *Grease*. Jimmy played the role of Kenickie. Billy became a mentor to Jimmy as well and wanted him to grow up to become a man of God. He spent many hours just listening and guiding Jimmy in his spiritual walk.

At Christmas in 1986, Billy returned to Wood Riverview Baptist Church to direct a full-length Christmas production called *The Greatest Gift of All*. It was in this small church that only a few months earlier his mother had accepted Christ. In this same wooden chapel between Ft. Blackmore and Dungannon, Virginia, Billy had performed in his first play (a Christmas production) at age four. From the role of a tiny little angel to directing this production, Billy felt that he had come full circle. Now, Billy was directing his family (sister, cousins, aunts, and uncles) in this production about Jesus.

Who would ever have thought that Billy would be back here? Something drew him back to the little chapel in the Appalachian Mountains. He felt a great need to give back to those who had encouraged him. He felt it was time to connect and plant some seeds among his family members.

Every night of the production, the small chapel was packed. People came from everywhere. Aunts, uncles and cousins that never went to church came to see their family members perform. The spirit of God seemed to draw them from the hollows to the little chapel they had all visited as children. God moved in a mighty way upon the congregation each evening. Souls were being saved and lives changed.

For Billy Wayne, the greatest joy of the production was seeing his youngest brother, Shannon, receive Christ into his heart. While casting the play, Billy felt led to ask Shannon to be a part of the production. Shannon never attended church on a regular basis and seemed to have no interest in "churchy stuff." Billy felt that this might be a way to get Shannon involved in something that would ultimately change his life. He knew that Shannon had a sensitive heart and was open to listening to God.

Shannon committed to playing the role of the repentant thief on the cross. During the practices, God worked overtime on Shannon's receptive heart. During the invitation on the evening of the last performance, Shannon stepped off the cross, took Billy by the hand, and went to the altar. Billy prayed with Shannon as he received Christ into his heart that night.

God was beginning to honor Billy's prayers and his faithfulness. God had heard every prayer that Billy had prayed for his family. Billy was seeing the evidence of his faith in believing that God was going to change his family.

The year was coming to an end. After one year at Lees-McRae, Billy felt God's calling to move on. Working with troubled students had given Billy the background to minister to hurting people. The seed to use theatre in ministry was planted in his heart as well. Billy had no idea how God was putting together all the puzzle pieces.

- Chapter 16 -

Gifts for Ministry

With a new year at hand, Billy felt that God was beginning a new work in him. In January of 1987, he felt led to use his gifts as a director. He felt that God was asking him to return to Kingsport to his home church (Tabernacle Baptist Church) and produce an Easter production. Billy began writing his first full-length Easter musical production, called *Watch the Lamb*. He was hired by the church part-time to direct the production for Easter. Even though Billy loved the people at Tabernacle and was thankful for the spiritual foundation they had given him, he still felt a sense of bondage. He had experienced a true personal relationship with Jesus Christ during his years at Berea College. Over the years, his walk with the Lord could not be contained within the walls of legalism and the do's and don'ts of religion.

Billy gained a better understanding of what it was like to be on a church staff while working at Tabernacle. He realized that he could never play the politics that exist in most churches. He found himself holding to his personal convictions and being unable to be a pleaser. He was eager to let others know of the freedom they could have in Christ as a result of the things that God had shown him: not freedom to sin, but a freedom from legalism. Billy wanted them to know that living for Jesus and being a Christian was not about the length of a man's hair or whether a woman could wear pants. All in all, Billy was learning about ministry and how to apply his gifts and abilities to do God's Kingdom work. He was grateful for the opportunity to grow and learn. It was in this process that God was preparing Billy for evangelism. He began to have a burden not only for lost people, but also for churches (the body of Christ) to grow in their walk of faith.

The Easter production was well received. The response was beyond anyone's expectation, including Billy's. Lives were changed and people were moved to a deeper walk of faith. Those involved in the production experienced true ministry as the story of Christ was brought to life.

Billy started understanding how theatre can be a means for all ages to be involved in ministry. From the extremely talented to the most backward, each person had a part in the big picture, and each was vital to the performance. Cultivating local talent became a trademark for Billy. Teaching people to step outside their comfort zones to present the gospel was very rewarding.

When the Easter production ended, Billy found himself wanting even more to use his theatrical training with ministry. He began searching for outlets to cultivate his theatrical abilities and satisfy his hunger for evangelism in spreading the gospel. This search landed him an audition for the *Smoky Mountain Passion Play* in Townsend, Tennessee, in May of 1986. The *Passion Play* was based on the last week of Christ's life on earth. Billy read about the auditions for this professional production in his hometown newspaper, the *Kingsport Times News*. He had to prepare two monologues for his audition. This was something Billy was accustomed to doing, but at the same time, he was anxious to see what God would do through the audition.

Billy felt that God was showing him that he could once again use his theatrical talents. What Billy was willing to give up for full-time ministry, God began to give back. God knew that He could trust Billy now. Theatre was not Billy's drive or idol anymore. Jesus was, and Billy did not want that to ever change.

The audition held at Maryville High School in Maryville, Tennessee, was exciting for Billy. It reminded him of the numerous auditions that landed him the many roles in both scholastic and professional theatre. Billy was taken back to a time where auditions were as natural as breathing. He reminisced about the auditions for Kings Island and Silver Dollar City (now Dollywood). He recalled the nerve-wracking waiting, the callbacks, the rehearsals, and the grueling performances of all of his past performances.

But this time was different. It wasn't about Billy anymore. It was about bringing glory to his Savior by using his gifts to further the gospel. What a twist. Could God actually give Billy back what he was willing to give up in order to follow Christ?

Billy walked into this audition out of obedience to God. He asked from God only to do the best within his abilities and that God would shine through him. And so it was. Billy performed the monologues and sang a song. He left knowing that he had already accomplished what God had asked.

A few days later, Billy received a phone call from the director, Charles Reese, inviting him to come to Townsend to be an actor/singer in the *Smoky Mountain Passion Play*. Billy moved to Maryville to share a house with a few other actors. He was only paid a meager salary, but all his needs were met.

What Billy didn't know was that God was getting ready to open his eyes to a different side of theatre and ministry. Billy's naïveté was soon demolished. Sometimes God allows circumstances in our lives to show us what *not* to do.

The *Smoky Mountain Passion Play* was performed by a professional company at a beautiful amphitheatre tucked away in a hollow on Bethel Church Road in Townsend, Tennessee. When Billy came to rehearsal the first night, he was overcome by the beauty of the set and the backdrop of the Smoky Mountains. He looked forward to working in this incredible setting with a group of Christians that would present the gospel of Christ. However, reality soon set in, and Billy could see that this professional company had lost its vision.

Billy found himself among a very talented cast of actors and actresses. He was under the direction of a good director, Charles Reese, and a wonderful assistant director, James Meyers. But the whole show lacked one thing: Jesus. So much attention was paid to the craft of theatre, and so little was given to honor Christ.

By their own admission, 80 percent of the cast and crew did not believe in Christ. They had very few morals and had little concern about the material they were performing. Billy was shocked. It was nothing to hear profanity before someone entered the stage during the performances. Sin reigned over the amphitheatre. Billy was grieved. He knew in his heart how things should be. He couldn't understand how something like this could ever come to be.

One afternoon before rehearsal, Billy felt led to go to the amphitheatre to pray. He heard Christian music being played from a boom box on stage. He followed the music to a work area, where the technical director was working on the temple. Billy introduced himself to Mark Pedro, who also worked in the production as an actor/singer. Billy, in his candid manner, asked Mark if he were a Christian. Mark's response was affirming and warm. Billy was thrilled to find that Mark truly loved the Lord. Little did they know that this meeting would begin a relationship that would last a lifetime.

Watching the performances night after night, Billy began to have a burden for the cast and crew and started witnessing to them. He wanted each one to know of his personal relationship in Christ. He had no hesitancy in rebuking them and being bold in his witness before them.

While working on the *Passion Play*, James Meyers asked Billy to be a part of a vocal ensemble that performed before the production. Soon, Billy was asked to sing solos. This was out of his comfort zone. He was fine singing with others but very uncomfortable singing solos before a crowd of people every evening. However, Billy seized this as an opportunity to tell his fellow cast members and the patrons of his love for Christ. He knew that God was stretching him, and he was willing to go the distance at whatever God wanted him to do.

Something strange started taking place. Patrons and cast members started requesting songs for Billy to sing before the performances. His passion for Christ was shining through. Billy never considered himself as an inspirational soloist, but God was pushing him in that direction. Before long, Billy was singing a solo every evening before the performance. Patrons began to ask Billy if he would come to their church to sing. Billy wasn't sure what God was doing, but he was willing to follow wherever God led.

As the summer moved on, Billy found himself leading some of the cast members to a saving knowledge of Jesus Christ. By the end of the season, Billy felt the liberty to share with Charles Reese what God had laid on his heart. He told Charles that God was not pleased with the compromise that was taking place at the theatre. He said that God was going to hold Charles personally responsible for the spiritual welfare of the production. Billy challenged Charles to re-evaluate why he was directing the production if it were not going to bring glory to God.

Charles listened to everything Billy had to say and asked him to return for another season and play the role of John the Beloved. He told Billy that he needed him to be a part of a team, along with Mark Pedro and James Meyers, to help change things. James had the same burden as Billy, but Charles's personality seemed to squelch everything that James tried to do.

Charles realized changes needed to occur and wanted the production to return to what it was originally, but he needed the help of others to make it happen.

Billy left the meeting encouraged but he soon left the production. Billy knew that God was moving him on. He was anxiously awaiting what God had in store for him. The experience at the *Smoky Mountain Passion Play* was invaluable. Billy learned so many life lessons. He learned how to work in the midst of hypocrisy and honor God. He understood what weak leadership and compromise brings to ministry. Most of all, Billy learned how a Christian theatre should *not* be run. All these lessons were building blocks for the ministry that God was preparing for Billy.

During the run of the production in Townsend, Billy was approached by Chrissy Davis, his former singing partner, to go to Sunset Gap Community Center in Cosby, Tennessee. Chrissy's father, Bob Davis, was looking for a cultural arts director for the center. Billy met with Bob and was immediately offered the job on a trial basis.

Billy moved to Sunset Gap in September after the *Passion Play* season was over. Sunset Gap Community Center was located in the foothills of the Great Smoky Mountains, miles from the nearest town, and was reminiscent of the beautiful mountains and valley of Billy's home. The community was made up of mostly farmers and mill workers. They were a very gracious people and extremely kind to Billy, and they quickly adopted him as one of their own.

Billy moved into an old wooden dormitory across the street from the community center. The dorm used to serve as a small hospital and clinic. Billy lived in a small apartment downstairs. The building housed laborers who came to work in the local community in the summer. Now it was fall. Billy was alone in the residence, except for an occasional squirrel or mouse that would invade the upstairs bedrooms.

Billy immediately started renovating the small auditorium on the second floor of the community center. He built a wooden picture frame around the front of the stage in vaudeville fashion. He painted the stage area and hung black backdrops to allow actors to move backstage without being seen. He forged lighting out of tin cans saved from the lunch room and created a homemade dimmer board with the help of a local electrician. All of the stagecraft classes and summer internship programs at Berea College paid off. He learned to create something from nothing. The locals were happy to see this vision come to fruition.

Sunset Gap Community Center was on the county line between Sevier and Cocke counties. Two sets of stairs ran up the front of the building. One set ran from Sevier County, and the other from Cocke County. This allowed the local children to legally go to the school without crossing over the county lines.

This historical place became the home of Sunset Gap Community Playhouse. Billy brought different theatrical groups in to perform at the center and began rehearsals for his original Victorian musical, *Merry Christmas, with Love* (later to be called *The Merriest Christmas*). The grand opening was attended by city officials and the state representative. It was quite the buzz in the small community and the local towns of Newport and Cosby.

Billy began to develop deep relationships with the people there. They reminded him of his family and friends back home. He recalled his deep Appalachian roots and the importance of family, community, and simple faith in an incredible God. The community embraced Billy as a local. Even Betty and Tootie, the ladies that ran the thrift shop at the center, made Billy feel right at home with home-cooked meals of pinto beans and cornbread. Joyce Hogue, Sunset Gap's secretary, became one of Billy's supporters and friends. She loved Jesus and was a staple in Billy's spiritual walk while he was there.

Billy loved the area and people so much that he wanted his family back home to visit. He arranged for the cast of *The Greatest Gift of All* from Wood Riverview Baptist Church to come and perform at Sunset Gap. The production was well received and afforded Billy the opportunity to join the two worlds that he loved.

Mary Belle (Billy's grandmother) came to the performance and all of the other productions that followed. She found every occasion to visit Billy and encourage him. Aunt Berniece, Ruth Hensley, and Bethel were always up for a visit. Great things seemed to be happening. Billy imagined that he would stay at Sunset Gap for a while. After all, God was allowing Billy the opportunity to use his gifts for ministry. At the same time, Billy was singing more and more. Doors kept opening for him to be a solo Christian music artist. This made him a bit anxious, but he knew that if God was leading in that direction, then God would prepare him.

The warmth and joy that Billy was experiencing soon turned cold like the winter that was starting to approach in Sunset Gap. God began to shed light on hidden sins in the hearts of people associated with the center. Billy urged the board of directors of Sunset Gap Community Center to handle the situation, and he bowed out of the scene. The board wanted Billy to stay, but he declined the offer and sadly waved farewell to a blessed time with wonderful people that would never be forgotten. These people took a chance and believed in Billy. They allowed him to fulfill dreams that could only come true in that magical place tucked in the east Tennessee Smoky Mountains.

- *Chapter 17* -

Kingdom's Call

After spending Christmas at home in 1987, Billy was beginning to grow restless. He knew something was soon to emerge on the horizon. He had been staying with Monnie Baker, a widow, from Tabernacle Baptist Church. She always welcomed Billy's company and loved for him to visit when he could. Billy was making road trips back and forth to Sevier County, as God was opening doors for him there. He was busy singing and speaking on weekends and sharing his faith when given the opportunity. He wasn't certain what to do next except wait.

While working at the *Smoky Mountain Passion Play* in summer of 1987, new construction was underway at Tommy Bartlett's Water Show in Pigeon Forge, Tennessee. Billy would often drive from Townsend to Pigeon Forge on his days off from the *Passion Play*. He couldn't help but notice the enormous sign that said, "Coming Soon, the *Great Passion Play*."

Out of curiosity, Billy stopped in to find out that the *Great Passion Play* in Eureka Springs, Arkansas, was opening a sister production in Pigeon Forge. This new *Passion Play* in Tennessee would become America's largest outdoor theatre production. The property would consist of a 4,000-seat outdoor amphitheatre, a five-acre set, and hotel/resort. The complex would be called Kingdom Resort.

Billy was excited to see something of this magnitude come to the area. He knew that it would pose a threat to the Townsend production. Maybe it needed to. At the time, the Townsend show was Tennessee's longest running outdoor production. Maybe it was time for it to retire. Billy felt that the Townsend production had lost its original vision. Maybe this was God's way of moving things along.

Would Billy get to be a part of something like this? Would God give him the opportunity to use his gifts at this new site?

Mark Pedro and his girlfriend Shelley had already moved from Townsend to Pigeon Forge. Mark went to work at Kingdom Resort as the set artist and served on the technical crew. Shelley was also going to work at the resort once things were up and going.

Mark had stayed in touch with Billy throughout his time at Sunset Gap Community Center and through his road trips to Sevier County. Mark asked Billy to apply for a job at Kingdom Resort. Billy had already put in an application, but the management couldn't seem to find it. Billy submitted another application and résumé. He hoped that he might get to be an actor/singer in the production.

Billy was quickly called in for an interview. He sat in the executive office with the producers and a man named Dr. Welton. They asked a few questions about his education at Berea and his background in professional and amateur theatre. They told Billy that they had all the information they needed and that he would hear from them as things progressed.

Two days later, Billy received a call from Dr. Welton. He said that he had checked some references at Berea and other places. He stated that Billy came highly recommended, but that one negative comment was given. It was from Pat Bruner, a personal friend of Dr. Welton's that worked at Berea as the director of the Baptist Student Union. Pat had said that Billy had a "tendency to be a workaholic and didn't know when to slow down." Dr. Welton told Billy that was exactly what he was looking for and offered Billy the job of assistant director. Billy was overwhelmed. He hadn't expected anything like this to happen.

Billy would actually get to direct certain scenes, handle the scheduling of actors (totaling 570 men, women, and children), and supervise twelve drama coaches that would be assisting in this mass production. The five-acre set housed a $750,000 sound system, a Foy Fly System that ascended Jesus 175 feet across the sky, and an underground town that contained two wardrobe sections, four dressing rooms for sixty people each, two guard dressing rooms, and a dressing room for the actor playing Jesus. Each evening production would consist of 250 actors on the set, twelve Arabian horses, four camels, two horse-drawn chariots, four donkeys, a flock of doves, and a herd of sheep.

Replicas of the Temple of Jerusalem, Pilate's Palace, the Upper Room, the Sanhedrin Court, the Garden Tomb, and Golgotha were secured within thirty-foot-high stone walls and twenty-foot-high gates. The scenery and backdrop were breathtaking.

There was a crunch to get the production ready by the end of May. Auditions took place in the ballroom of the Kingdom Resort Hotel. People came from everywhere to be a part of the production. Dr. Welton and Billy conducted the auditions. After the leads were selected, the "cast of thousands" was divided into subgroups led by the twelve drama coaches.

Billy moved into a house in Pigeon Forge. It was an old log cabin that had been renovated into a two-story house at the end of a gravel road. Billy lived there with Mark Pedro. It provided a sanctuary for Billy. It was a great place to entertain family and friends from out of town.

Kingdom Resort was off to a great start. At the time, one of the most popular artists in Christian music, Sandi Patti, was the goodwill ambassador for the resort. Whenever she visited the resort, Billy was assigned as her liaison. It was a thrill for him to get to know someone in the Christian music industry. Billy also met her husband, John Helvering. Through Helvering, Billy would also meet with representatives of Impact Records. At the time, The Gaithers were heading the record company and were looking for new artists. This led to a proposed recording contract. Even though it was tempting, Billy turned them down. He felt it was something that God didn't want for him at the time.

Through his employment at Kingdom Resort, Billy met some wonderful people. He started attending Evergreen Church in Sevierville. This nondenominational church offered contemporary worship and awesome teaching and mentorship by Pastor Randy Davis. This was something Billy longed for and appreciated.

Billy also met a wonderful lady by the name of Marion Ausmus. Marion was one of the drama coaches. After she retired from banking on Wall Street, Marion and her husband moved from New Jersey to a chalet on Ski View Drive in Gatlinburg, Tennessee. Marion boasted that she had the highest private residence on her mountain, which was a part of the Great Smoky Mountain National Forest. Her property bordered the National Park.

After getting to know Billy, Marion, whose husband had passed away, would often invite Billy to her mountain chalet for dinner and conversation. They had deep discussions about their faith in a loving God. Marion was originally from Germany and came from a Lutheran background. She had a strong faith in God but had missed out on her personal relationship with Jesus. As a drama coach, she was in charge of over fifty actors each evening. The cast call (before the show) began with devotions led by the different actors.

Marion had shared with Billy that those devotions changed her walk with God. When the actors shared their hearts, she could see the love of Jesus more than anything she had ever experienced before. She longed to have that kind of relationship with Christ.

Through those devotions and long talks with Billy, she met Christ in a very personal way. She also mentored Billy in many ways. She was a woman of dignity, integrity, and class. She had been on Broadway as a child and had performed throughout her life. She knew how to entertain people. She had a love for old movies and musicals and took every occasion to feed into Billy's young life. She shared so many stories and experiences. Billy took in every word.

Whenever Broadway shows came to Knoxville, Marion made sure they attended. They would go to shows and productions and critique the performances. She poured her energy into the life of a young man she believed would help change the world. The friendship they shared was invaluable.

Marion got to know Billy's family. She especially loved Mary Belle, Billy's grandmother. She took it upon herself to spoil Mary Belle, who often went with Billy to visit Marion on her mountain and find refuge from the busy outside world.

By midsummer, things at Kingdom Resort started heating up. The production was doing well, but the infrastructure was falling apart. The production company from Eureka Springs was in disagreement with the owners of the resort, Ed Neely and Jess Davis. They were constantly feuding over logistics. While this was going on, Dr. Welton, Billy, and the cast kept doing their jobs. Every evening, they shared the gospel of the life of Christ with thousands of people, who were unaware of the battles that were being fought behind closed doors in the administrative offices.

Dr. Welton was also a professor at Carson Newman College and had planned to turn the reins over to Billy by the fall semester. Dr. Welton was a true mentor and had taught Billy more than he could ever learn in a classroom. He picked up where Paul Power (Billy's college mentor) had left off. At age twenty-five, Billy would soon become the director of America's largest outdoor drama production. Dr. Welton made Billy confident to take on the task.

Tempers flared between Eureka Springs and Pigeon Forge. Dr. Welton somehow ended up in the middle. In order to protect innocent people involved, he stepped back into his role as professor at Carson Newman as the war raged on. Eventually, the *Great Passion Play* producers pulled out, leaving behind a devastated cast and crew. Most cast members had no idea what had occurred nor what would happen next. Billy felt that it was his responsibility to hold them together. He knew that the cast wasn't interested in the politics of the situation. They simply wanted to continue sharing Christ through the drama.

Billy was secured by the owners of the resort as the director of *Christmas at the Kingdom*. This production would debut in November at the Kingdom Resort. The production would consist of a live Nativity drive-through with different scenes depicting the events leading to the birth of Christ. It also consisted of "Fantasy Valley of Lights," which boasted hundreds of thousands of Christmas lights and figurines. Those attending could get out of their cars and enjoy the holiday sights from the concession area while listening to local choirs and musical artists.

While tension was building between the executive offices, Billy kept the morale of the cast together as he plowed through the Christmas season. Just when he thought that everything was fine, another monster reared its ugly head. Billy named it "Greed" and did everything in his power to keep it away from his cast.

Neely and Davis began to fight among themselves. Neely was ministry-minded, and Davis was money-minded. Accusations flew back and forth during the whole Christmas season. Finally, they decided to part ways and Neely bowed out. Billy was left once again to hold the cast and crew together. The remaining owner, Jess Davis, became paranoid and began grasping for straws to hold everything together. Billy noticed that Davis was making unwise decisions and felt led by the Holy Spirit to confront him.

On January 7, 1989, Billy told Davis that God wasn't pleased with what was going on at Kingdom Resort. He told him that if things didn't change, God would close the doors and that he would lose everything. Billy felt the liberty to leave Kingdom Resort that day, even though he grieved at the loss. Billy searched his soul that day and thought, "*What a wonderful opportunity these men had to reach thousands for Christ, and they blew it. God, what are they thinking? Why did You bring me here? What are You trying to teach me? This seemed to be the perfect situation. Why did this have to happen?*"

Working at Kingdom Resort had afforded Billy the opportunity to go away on weekends for concerts and retreats. Billy met thousands of people who passed through Kingdom Resort, and many of them asked him to come to their church and share his ministry of music and speaking. Billy had already booked ministry events through March.

When Billy left Kingdom Resort, he stepped out in faith into full-time evangelism. Billy's prophetic message came true for the resort; it struggled over the next season and shut its doors before fall of the same year. It grieved Billy and all who had the privilege of being a part of it.

Billy never looked back. The Lord began a new adventure in his life. Billy knew in his heart that he had to follow God no matter the cost. He asked God what it was that He wanted him to do. God said, "I want you to sing and share your faith."

"But God, I don't really sing that well," Billy replied. He knew that he could sell a Broadway tune to an audience. He knew that he could sing in a group. He could even share Scripture and his faith. But to sing … solo … what was God thinking? Nevertheless, Billy surrendered to God's call to full-time ministry.

The first concert to mark Billy's commission was presented on a Saturday evening at Evergreen Church in Sevierville, Tennessee. Billy shared Christ through music and testimony and saw three new souls ushered into the Kingdom of God. The next morning after the worship service, Pastor Randy Davis asked to see Billy in his office. Randy shared how much he loved him and that he admired everything he was doing. Randy then said, "Billy, you are a true man of God. I know how much God uses you. That was evident by last night's concert. However, I feel I need to tell you that music is not your strong point. Your voice is okay, but you are real 'pitchy,' and you're not that great a singer. Perhaps you need to reconsider what you think God is showing you."

Billy was devastated. He wasn't upset with Randy, who had always been one of his biggest supporters. He was upset that God was asking him to do something that he felt he wasn't capable of to begin with. Was God trying to humiliate him?

Billy sat in his packed car and cried for a few minutes. He began to ask God what to do. God was not interested in his ability but in his obedience. It dawned on Billy that if he would ever succeed at this, that it would have to be all God. It took little faith for Billy to act or direct a play; he could do those things easily. These were talents that God had given him. To speak his heart in front of a group was also innate to his nature. But God had asked Billy to sing as a soloist. This would require faith beyond talent. God whispered to him, "Billy, I am going to take your weakest ability and use it for My glory. You will never be able to claim any glory for yourself for singing. Every time you stand to sing, you will be utterly dependent on Me to get you through. You will use your other gifts, but this is what I am calling you to."

Peace swept through Billy as he started his car and headed to perform a concert at another church that evening. When he stood that night, he knew what it was like to be a vessel for God. He knew that God would have to give him the confidence and ability to stand once more. God was more than faithful. Billy finally knew what it was like to be absolutely dependent upon God for everything. By the end of March, Billy had so many bookings that he no longer needed another job. Everywhere he went, God opened new doors for him.

- *Chapter 18* -

Tell Them

Throughout the years that followed, Billy often wondered why people listened to his music or bought his albums. He loved to sing and share the gospel but always stood in humble adoration of a God that would use anything or anybody to declare His glory. God always honored Billy's obedience, for obedience is greater than sacrifice.

As Billy was starting his full-time ministry, God was working on Steve Griffith. Steve had met and married Jenny Smith. Steve had been called to become a pastor, and he and Jenny moved to Wake Forest, North Carolina, to attend Southeastern Theological Seminary.

Steve and Jenny's home became a base for Billy's ministry over the next few years. Billy networked with many pastors from the seminary and surrounding areas. God kept expanding his ministry. It was here in Wake Forest that Billy wrote his first song.

Late one evening as Billy, Steve, and Jenny were relaxing and discussing the events of the day, Billy received a phone call from his mother. He sensed something was wrong because she was phoning so late in the evening, but he couldn't imagine what the problem might be. Things were going so well for her since Hubert Brock had come into her life, and Billy was continually amazed at how God was using Brock to help Bethel grow in her walk of faith. Bethel's life and home were so different now, so what could be the problem? It was Billy's brother, Randy. Randy had threatened suicide that night; he locked himself in the bathroom and had asked to talk with Billy on the phone.

After a long phone conversation with his brother, Randy emerged from the bathroom to be embraced and encouraged by a loving mother and stepfather. This would be the first of many episodes of depression that Randy would battle over the next few years.

Once again, Billy had made everyone feel okay. God had allowed him to be used to offer hope to a hopeless soul. It was different this time. When Billy hung up the phone, his mind raced to find answers for himself. He thought, *I travel all over the United States telling everyone about Jesus. Have I failed to be there and tell my own family?*

God took Billy to Ezekiel 33:7–9:

> *Son of man, I have made you a watchman for the house of Israel; so hear the word I speak and give them warning from me. When I say to the wicked, "O wicked man, you will surely die," and you do not speak out to dissuade him from his ways, that wicked man will die for his sin, and I will hold you accountable for his blood. But if you do warn the wicked man to turn from his ways and he does not do so, he will die for his sin, but you will have saved yourself.*

That night, Billy had a vision of the rapture. He woke up and penned the words to "Tell Them":

Late one night while I lay dreaming
Came a vision to my mind
Some of my loved ones stood there crying
Jesus had come and left them here behind

Holy Spirit come and woo them
To the Father up above
Blessed Jesus you can save them
Through the power of your love

Then before me stood my daddy
Tears were streaming down his face
"You did not tell me about Jesus
About His love and of His saving grace"

Then I saw my younger brother
His arms were reaching to the sky
"Please, Lord Jesus, take me with you
No one told me," was his cry

Holy Spirit come and woo them
To the Father up above
Blessed Jesus you can save them
Through the power of your love

Then from sleep I was awakened
Realized what I had done
I had failed to tell my loved ones
About Jesus, God's begotten Son

I fell right down before my Savior
"Please forgive me, Lord," I pray.
"I need to tell them about salvation
Lord, please give me all the words to say"

Holy Spirit come and woo them
To the Father up above
Blessed Jesus you can save them
Through the power of your love

The next day, Billy couldn't get the words out of his mind. It was like a broken record repeating itself over and over again. All day long, the words kept echoing in his heart.

Later in the day, Billy was at Steve and Jenny's getting ready for a revival that was being held at Holly Grove Baptist Church, where Steve was pastor. Billy was in the shower, singing the song, when Steve overheard him and asked him to sing the song at the revival that evening. Billy was very reluctant to sing the song. He felt the song had been given to him by God and wasn't sure it was good enough for others to hear. Steve assured him that the song was good and that it needed to be sung for the revival. Steve promised that he wouldn't tell anyone that Billy wrote the song beforehand. Billy was hesitant but agreed. Maybe God did want him to share the song that night. Someone attending the revival might need to hear the same message that God had given him.

When the service started that night, Billy was unusually nervous. He had been singing before audiences for some time now, but he had never shared a song that he had written. When it came time to sing, Billy let the words fall on the hearts of the people, just as God had given the song to him. When he finished singing, people throughout the congregation were crying. When Steve announced to the crowd that Billy had written the song, the audience was floored. That which seemed to be such a simple truth to Billy turned out to be a big blessing to others.

"Tell Them" became Billy's signature song. Everywhere he went, people wanted him to share his testimony and share the song. It was rereleased in the late 1990s and enabled Billy to become a regional finalist for Spotlight Song of the Year with the Gospel Music Association (GMA) in Atlanta. Perhaps the greatest reward was when he sang this song in concert when his family attended.

Through songwriting, Billy understood even more about the power of words and music. This simple song was the first of many that God would inspire Billy to write over the years. He would never fully understand why or how God could use him to communicate the message of Christ through song. What Billy felt was one of his weakest abilities, God would use for His glory.

In the spring of 1990, Marion Ausmus had a burden to see Billy record a music project. After going to several concerts, Marion felt that people would benefit if they could listen to Billy's music whenever they wanted. She knew that God wanted her to fund a music project. After much prayer and convincing, Billy went to Nashville to record his first album. He met up with his old friend and music partner, Chrissy Davis (now Chrissy Davis-Camp). While making the album, Billy had the opportunity to work at the Nashville Playhouse Theatre as technical director. Billy was in charge of the set design and artistic direction for the musical *Annie*. He also played the supporting role of Drake, the butler. Working at the Nashville Playhouse paid for his expenses while living in Nashville. It also earned him a technical achievement award and recognition by critics as a credible actor in the Nashville area.

While in Nashville, Billy and Chrissy would help lead in praise and worship at Christ Community Church in Franklin. Billy felt it strange to be leading worship with Steve Green, Michael Card, Whiteheart, and other artists in the congregation, yet it never fazed him from accomplishing God's call. Billy learned a great deal under Pastor Scotty Smith. He also frequented a Bible study led by singer/songwriter Michael Card and attended Koinonia, a contemporary nondenominational worship service. It was often led by popular Christian artists like Michael W. Smith and Amy Grant. God was expanding Billy spiritually and musically. His eyes and heart were being opened to so many avenues and ministry possibilities, and he was enjoying every step of the journey.

The recording project ended at the same time the run of *Annie* was over. Even though Billy loved Nashville and the opportunities that were being opened to him, it was time for him to move on. He moved back to Kingsport to set up a ministry headquarters. He renovated his mother's basement by removing an old furnace and putting in a bedroom and den. This would give him a place to sleep and to work when he found the occasion to come home.

Billy's music ministry expanded until he was on the road about forty-eight weeks out of the year. God continued to use Billy in spite of what others thought or said. Billy was learning more every day to depend on God. He became a true itinerant minister, traveling from one church to another, sharing the message of the gospel and the hope of Jesus Christ. Billy learned to listen as God spoke. The sky was the limit. All that Billy wanted was to be faithful to his calling.

- *Chapter 19* -

Opened Doors

God honored Billy's step of faith over the next few years. He was asked to share in music and testimony at Fullerton Evangelical Free Church (E.V. Free) in Fullerton, California, where Chuck Swindoll was pastor. Chuck had been an inspiration to Billy for many years. Steve Griffith's brother, Jim, had started attending the church when he moved to California. Jim had married Jeanette Miniaci, whose family attended E.V. Free. Jeanette's sister, Michelle, worked at the church and introduced the staff to Billy Wayne's ministry. Billy was asked to come back on several occasions.

On one visit to Chuck's church, Billy was approached by another record label. They had been representing mostly Hispanic artists and wanted to expand into other markets. They wanted to represent Billy and help his music ministry move forward. Their contract promised audiences and venues of no fewer than two thousand people. They would set the price for Billy's appearances and would also act as a management company.

Billy was reminded of his promise to God not to charge for the gospel. He also wanted to be able to go to the smaller churches and introduce them to Christian music. He didn't want a record company that was going to control so many aspects of the ministry with no input from him. Needless to say, Billy reluctantly declined the enticing offer; he knew that God had other plans.

A couple of years later, Michelle Miniaci moved to Nashville to work for *dc Talk* at True Artist Management. While visiting Nashville, Billy had the opportunity to meet the guys from dc Talk and to watch them record in their studio. Billy admired their stand for Christ and their passion for music and ministry. While he attended Gospel Music Association Week, Billy stayed at Michael Tate's house. While he was grateful to meet these famous people, Billy was never star struck. He only felt that God was allowing him to see what the Christian music industry was like from the inside out.

In the early to mid-90s, Billy spent a great deal of time in the Myrtle Beach area of South Carolina. Several youth groups that Billy worked with wanted him to lead retreats for them there. He spent much of the summer doing just that. While working in Myrtle Beach, Billy was introduced to Geof Kimber of the Myrtle Beach Opry, an incredibly talented musician and singer. Geof was originally from Papua, New Guinea, but he had come over to America with a missionary to do some evangelism and realized God was calling him to stay. Geof and his wife Tanya settled in the Myrtle Beach area to start his ministry.

Billy had been looking for a new producer. God's timing was perfect. After being introduced, Billy and Geof hit it off immediately. Geof produced three recording projects for him. Billy encouraged Geof to step out in faith into music evangelism. Geof and Tanya sold all they had and went on the road full time. Billy and Geof had many opportunities to work together over the following years.

During this same time, while doing a great deal of ministry in the Wake Forest area, Billy met Julia Ledford, the youth director at a local church. Billy had the opportunity to work with Julia on several different occasions. Julia took Billy under her wing and helped push his ministry forward.

In 1994, after being involved in Billy's ministry, Julia felt that it was time for him to start a nonprofit tax-exempt corporation. She was willing to foot the bill for the legal fees and undertake the painstaking process to get it done.

At this same time, Billy was still working out of his mother's basement in Kingsport. He had been praying for God to send some administrative help. The paperwork, booking, and correspondence were too much for one person to handle. Billy was overwhelmed with all the responsibilities of the administrative aspects of his ministry. Bethel tried to help with the correspondence and booking, but the workload was too much. It was evident that something needed to be done. The ministry needed space and people to expand its efforts. Billy found himself sitting in the basement one night, calling on God for help. He hated knowing that valuable time was being consumed working on the business aspects of running a ministry; he felt discouraged. *Why can't I just tell people about Jesus?* he thought. *Why does this have to be so complicated? I need to spend my time and efforts in the Word and with God and not on all this paperwork.*

Billy's Uncle Howard and Aunt Berniece lived next door to Bethel. There was a small four-room house on their property that was used to store hay for the calf that was running around in the fenced-in yard. Howard offered the house to Billy to use as a ministry office. Billy couldn't believe his uncle's generosity. Billy and his family went to work immediately and renovated the house into office space.

Seeing all that was happening around Billy, his cousin Terry knew that God was calling her to the ministry. She volunteered her time at the office, as did her sister, Debora. Bethel continued helping with the financial affairs. Other family and friends would do their share as the ministry enlisted their help on occasion.

Julia's burden grew stronger. Billy's workload did the same. God used Julia to start something great in Billy's life. Vision Productions Inc., Billy Wayne Ministries was born in the spring of 1995. The founding members of the executive board consisted of Billy Wayne, Julia Ledford, Karen Richards Patrick, Steve Griffith, and Brian Prather.

Billy and the executive board began to pray for administrative staff and office workers. God began working quickly in orchestrating this prayer request.

Leigh Meredith, from Williamstown, West Virginia, had attended one of Billy's singles retreats. God changed her and seized her heart. She began to help organize events throughout West Virginia. She gave as much time as she could to see the ministry succeed. When the position of business administrator came around, Leigh was more than ready. She was currently enrolled at West Virginia University at Parkersburg, and Billy had already teased her about coming on staff when she graduated.

Through the leading of the Holy Spirit, Leigh yielded to God and headed for Kingsport. The Lord opened up the opportunity for her to finish her degree in business from East Tennessee State University (ETSU), in neighboring Johnson City. She became a full-time student at ETSU while working full-time for the ministry. Karen Patrick opened her home to Leigh, and God provided for her needs through a faith-based salary from Vision Productions.

Billy's schedule continued to get even busier. Other staff members were added. Terry began to work full-time as office assistant. Connie McMullins soon joined the ranks as merchandising director. Michelle Miniaci moved from True Artist Management in Nashville to do public relations for the team. The small house was renovated once more by adding room in the basement. Volunteers increased, as did staff members.

Soon, Brad and Susan Owens from Henderson, North Carolina, came on staff. Susan became the financial administrator, and Brad was the bus driver and maintenance supervisor. Billy's busy schedule put him on the road for forty-nine weeks out of the year. His bus became his home away from home. Life on the road was quite hectic.

Billy was also balancing time in Eden, North Carolina, where Steve Griffith moved after finishing the seminary. From 1992 to 2003, Billy worked with Osborne Baptist Church to produce several musical passion plays (*Watch the Lamb, The Light of Life, Once for All,* and *More than Just a Man*). Each year, three months prior to the annual Easter production for the church, Billy would rehearse during the weekdays while still traveling every weekend with his music ministry. Billy gained some wonderful relationships with the people at Osborne Baptist Church. They became his family and a spiritual backbone for him.

When Billy first started the musical productions at Osborne, Jill and George "Peanut" Gauldin offered their hospitality and opened their home to Billy. Others, like Jean Slaughter and Frances DeHart, were prayer warriors for the ministry. After three years, Ray and Juanita Robertson (Jean and Frances's parents) offered an attic apartment for Billy to live in while working on the production. The apartment provided privacy and rest for Billy, as his schedule stretched him physically and spiritually. Juanita's home-cooked meals were always a welcome sight after being on the road. Ray's stories and humor drew Billy away from his frustrations with his hectic life on the road. The Robertsons became Billy's second family and ministered to him over the twelve years of theatre ministry at Osborne Baptist Church.

The Easter productions grew over the years. From a small sanctuary that held only about 180 people to one that held over 800, the productions became well known as one of the best around. The plays were Billy's original works. They were professionally staged on a 2,000-square-foot set and costumed by a crew of seamstresses and wardrobers. With a cast and crew of over two hundred, these productions became everything that Billy felt that he had left behind with professional theatre.

In 2000, while Billy was working on the Easter production at Osborne, Bill Hybels from Willow Creek Community Church in Chicago contacted him. They wanted him to come to Willow Creek and play the part of Jairus in their Easter musical production. This was a huge production that would reach thousands for Christ. They offered to fly Billy back and forth and to pay him a considerable amount of money to play the part. After much prayer, Billy realized that he had already made a commitment to Osborne and that his integrity was at stake. He declined the offer and stayed at Osborne. Once again, Billy wanted to do what God wanted instead of following a dream. God honored Billy's obedience once more with a great harvest of ministry. When people heard that Billy had declined Willow Creek's offer to play Jairus, they donated the same amount of money to Billy's ministry. Billy was learning once again that in God's eyes, obedience is greater than sacrifice.

Throughout his years in ministry, Billy had learned that it was important to reinvent himself when working with teenagers. He knew the importance of keeping current with music. He always surrounded himself with people and artists that were better than him.

One such group was Jamie and Jennifer. Billy had booked them to perform at Beach Week, a conference held in Myrtle Beach that Billy started in order to consolidate some of the summer camps that he was doing.

Jamie and Jennifer became good friends of Billy's and encouraged him to talk to their producer, Dan Mukala. Jamie played one of Dan's songs for Billy. The song, "He Walked a Mile in My Shoes," was recorded later that year by Christian music artist Clay Crosse. Billy was impressed by Dan's production of Jamie and Jennifer's projects, and when he heard the song, he wanted to meet him. Billy and Dan talked on the phone, and Dan agreed to produce Billy's next album.

During this same time, Dan was getting quite a bit of recognition. He was an established songwriter and was producing tracks for many major artists. Dan proved to be a great friend with an incredible talent, and he was able to bring many of Billy's songs to life. Out of this, the "Abandoned to God" music project was birthed. Dan was an inspiration and supporter to Billy, both personally and professionally.

Billy and Dan's friendship flourished over the years. Dan performed with Billy at Beach Week on a few occasions, and their friendship became very strong. Dan's career was taking off, and so was Billy's ministry. Time and schedules kept them apart, but they continued to stay in each other's lives over the months and years to follow.

It was time for Billy to make another album. Dan Mukala had signed with Essential Records. His career had soared but other aspects of his life, mainly his marriage, were crashing. Dan and Billy would spend time on the phone in prayer and conversation. Dan had no time to produce a full project for Billy but agreed to help him with the music tracks and artistic direction.

Billy started once again on a quest to find a producer. He had placed some of his music in listening rooms on the Internet. The entire Vision Production staff had been praying for God to send a new producer. One day, Scotty Wilbanks of the Christian group New Song sent Billy an e-mail. He had heard Billy's music and was interested in producing his next recording. Billy explained the situation concerning Dan and asked Scotty if he would be willing to produce the vocals and complete all post-production. Scotty agreed, and the collaboration was a success. Together, Billy, Scotty, and Dan produced *The Call*.

Over the next couple of years, Dan grew discouraged and went through a divorce. He had stepped away from Essential Records in order to save his marriage, but it was to no avail. Billy encouraged Dan to keep on keepin' on. Dan had two sons to raise, and a whole lot of work was still coming his way as a songwriter and producer. God used Dan's trials to make him a better man. Time, distance, and schedules kept Billy and Dan from working together on the next project, but the bond they shared would be a staple of encouragement for both of them throughout the years.

Dan had the opportunity to write songs for many Christian music artists. Many of his songs charted, and he even won nominations as Songwriter of the Year. Dan would go on to write for secular artists as well, including the Backstreet Boys and Nick Lachey. God was using Dan, and Billy was proud to know him as a friend and confidant.

Billy and Scotty Wilbanks went on to work together on in producing another album, entitled *Act of God*. It was the first time that Scotty had produced both the music and vocals for Billy. They had to learn to work with each other in a give-and-take game. Scotty had a way of stretching Billy outside his comfort zone as an artist. They became close friends during the production of the project, which eventually opened doors far beyond either of their expectations.

- *Chapter 20* -

Oh Ye, of Little Faith

Nineteen ninety-seven proved to be one of the best years of Billy's life. Cecil had seen many changes in Billy's ministry. He had seen the changes in Bethel and how God had blessed her with a loving husband. Brock, Bethel, and Billy had been praying for God to bring change in Cecil and his wife, Lois. God did just that. Lois's heart was changed first. Her daughter Andrea had been praying for her, and Lois could no longer run from God. She had given her life to God when she was younger, but she had been on the run for a long time. Lois began to seek after God. She renewed her faith and commitment and immediately joined the others in praying for Cecil's salvation.

God was still mending the father/son relationship between Billy and Cecil. Billy was now able to talk openly and honestly to Cecil about Jesus. One night after "Yuletide," a Christmas show produced by Vision Productions in Kingsport, Cecil phoned Billy. Cecil had been at the concert that evening and when he called Billy, Billy knew the Holy Spirit had been weighing heavy on Cecil's heart. Ever since Maudie died, Cecil had been soul searching.

Two years earlier during Christmas of 1995 the family gathered at the house of Cecil's sister, Betty Jo. As they were sitting in the living room singing, Cecil found himself sitting at Maudie's feet. He had always loved and adored his mother. She then asked Billy to come and sit beside her and sing "Tell Them." Cecil and the rest of the family had heard the song many times, and it had become a family favorite. Because of Billy's commitment to Christ and obvious sacrifice for ministry, many in the

Arrington family had become Christians. Christmas get-togethers, which were once dreaded, were now joyful occasions. As Christ began to change the lives of family members, the holiday season began to be a celebration of the entire family's faith in Christ.

The Spirit of God was in their midst as Billy sang his signature song. Cecil was moved beyond words and began to cry in front of the family, who could sense the room was filled with the Holy Spirit. When the song was over, Maudie was holding Billy's and Cecil's hands. She said, "Billy, whatever you do, don't stop praying for your daddy. When I'm gone, don't stop praying." Billy promised her and faithfully fulfilled that promise. On September 15, 1996, one month prior to her ninety-third birthday, Maudie went home to be with the Lord.

In the two years that followed, the Holy Spirit worked overtime on Cecil's heart. Even in the passing of his mother, Cecil had no anger toward God. Maybe there was a calming sense in knowing that she would be reunited with his father, Enoch. Maybe Cecil was getting tired of fighting the Holy Spirit. Regardless, Cecil was broken and humbled.

The phone call from Cecil after the Yuletide production was an answer to prayer. Cecil spilled his heart. He shared about his father, Enoch. He told Billy that he was bitter toward the Christian men that let his father die. He said that he couldn't understand why God would take his Christian father. Cecil shed a thousand tears that night. Billy listened intently, as he was getting a better understanding of what Cecil had felt for years.

When Billy hung up the phone, he was amazed. He knew now that God had been at work even when Billy couldn't see what was happening. He knew that for his dad to be that vulnerable meant that Cecil trusted Billy. He knew a wall had been removed between them that had been standing unmovable for years. Now that wall was nothing but rubble lying at the feet of Jesus.

Billy had grown accustomed to seeing Cecil at his evangelical events. When Cecil first started coming, it was to outdoor concerts or in nonchurch settings. Cecil might even sit in his car or stand apart from the crowd to watch a concert. Eventually, he would timidly enter the church houses and sit inconspicuously in the back. Cecil edged his way nearer the front as the years passed. He began crying through the whole concert, not caring what others thought of his being there.

Billy knew that God was working on Cecil. He had a promise from Scripture that God would save his father. Perhaps this would be the day. At times Billy doubted. He had been praying for twenty-seven years for his father's salvation. Was God listening? *Why won't Daddy yield to the Lord?* Billy thought. *I know God is wearing him out. Why doesn't he just give in? Would he let pride stand in the way of his salvation?*

On December 7, 1997, Billy was doing a small concert at Heritage Baptist Church, his Aunt Betty Jo's church in Hiltons, Virginia. This night was different. Cecil came in with camera in tow (it had become his unofficial duty to video every concert Billy gave because the grandchildren loved to watch the videos when they spent the night at Cecil and Lois's). Cecil stood in the far left aisle of the church, close to the front, to be near an electrical outlet for the camera. As the service progressed, so did the Spirit of God. At the end of each concert, Billy always asked for people to stand if they had a need, whether financially, emotionally, spiritually, or physically. This night people stood throughout the sanctuary. Billy couldn't help noticing his dad. Cecil had his hand raised to indicate he had a need. Billy asked the Christians in the audience to move to these people and offer words of prayer and encouragement.

Billy saw his stepmother Lois go to Cecil. He then saw Bethel and Brock go to Cecil. God had bridged a huge gap between Billy's parents. They had become good friends over the years. He knew that this was a miracle in itself; only God could fix all the messiness that had occurred between Cecil and Bethel.

When Billy saw the pastor of the church move over to Cecil, he panicked. He knew that Cecil couldn't stand preachers. The pastor quickly prayed and moved back to his seat. Billy whispered a quiet "Thank you" to Jesus. Cecil and the others returned to their seats when everyone had finished praying with them. Billy then offered an invitation for people to come forward to pray. He extended the invitation to those who needed a personal relationship with Jesus Christ.

As Billy was praying, he began to sing the words, "I've been washed in the blood of the crucified Lamb." At that moment, Billy looked up, and standing before him was his father. Billy began to whisper, "Oh ye, of little faith. God help my unbelief. Can this be real? Is Daddy standing here for salvation?"

Billy looked at his father, who was broken and crying. "Daddy, what did you come for?" Billy needed to hear his response.

Cecil answered, "You've prayed long enough, son. I need Jesus."

Billy knelt down with his dad and introduced Cecil to his best friend and Savior, Jesus Christ. The whole church erupted in rejoicing. God's

Spirit fell on that church. It was a time of great celebration. All the years of pain and prayer began to make sense.

Cecil took the microphone from Billy. This shocked Billy because Cecil wasn't the type to talk in public. Cecil's burley voice uttered, "For over forty years, I have wasted my life. I've hurt a lot of people and made a lot of mistakes. Now, I will spend the rest of my life tellin' people what Jesus has done for me."

And that's just what Cecil did. He became one of Billy's greatest supporters. He became Billy's biggest inspiration and hero. God began an unbelievable work in Cecil's life and heart. God not only saved Cecil but called him to something even greater than anyone could imagine.

In the following years, Cecil would go to Mexico on mission trips with Billy. He would kneel at the altar on many occasions as Billy gave the invitation. Cecil would pray with others to receive Jesus into their hearts as Lord and Savior.

Vision Productions hosts many retreats throughout the year. Cecil volunteers as kitchen staff to help Billy. At a retreat soon after Cecil's salvation, Billy was having a consecration service where he asked people to go to someone they had hurt and make things right. Billy saw his dad approaching him with tear-filled eyes and a look of remorse on his face.

Billy asked, "What are you doing?"

Cecil answered, "I have to do this. I need to tell you that I am sorry for the way I treated you as a child. I wasn't a good daddy and I hurt you. I need you to forgive me."

"Daddy, when you asked Jesus in your heart, it was over. You don't owe me anything. I forgave you a long time ago."

They embraced that day, father and son, unguarded and restored. Billy felt like a child again, seeking and receiving the approval of the greatest man he knew. Cecil was a proud father. The unforgiving chains of bitterness and regret now lay at the feet of Jesus.

In June of 2005 at Beach Week in Myrtle Beach, South Carolina, Billy had the great honor of baptizing his father in the ocean. Everyone there was touched by this wonderful display of God's victory and healing. And God was watching.

- *Chapter 21* -

Sacred Mountains

Growth brings change. Nineteen ninety-eight was a year for great changes in Billy Wayne's life and ministry. In the spring of that year, Vision Productions moved its headquarters to Broad Street in downtown Kingsport. The small cottage in East Carter's Valley could no longer hold the growing demands of Billy Wayne Ministries. The ministry move enabled Vision Productions' staff to share office space with Ground Zero, a ministry formed by Scott Payseur to care for the youth of the Tri-Cities area (Kingsport, Johnson City, and Bristol). Billy's executive board agreed to partner with Ground Zero until they secured their nonprofit tax-exempt status. The office space marriage was a success.

About the same time, one of Leigh's friends, Jill Buckles, joined the ministry team as financial administrator. Brad and Susan had moved on to work for Harvest Home, a children's home in Duffield, Virginia, just north of Kingsport, before working in the ministry at Celebration Church in Kingsport.

Jill also hailed from the great state of West Virginia and had been a part of the same singles ministry from Williamstown as Leigh. Billy had met both Leigh and Jill on the same retreat in West Virginia. Jill always had a great respect for Billy and wanted to help in a greater way. She married Curtis Buckles and moved to Elizabethton, Tennessee. The door opened for her to come to the ministry. Jill became a great asset to the ministry and a faithful supporter of Billy.

As the staff was changing, so was Billy's vision for the ministry. He had already begun to add musicians in order to form a full band to travel with him. He had a desire to mentor others to use their music abilities for ministry.

The day before Mother's Day in 1999, Mary Belle Salling passed away at the age of eighty-five. This was a blow to Billy. His grandmother had been there for him through the years. Even though she had been suffering and he knew that her homecoming to heaven would be great, he wanted her to be around just a little longer. There were so many things that he wanted her to see, so many songs he wanted her to hear. Being on the road was difficult for Billy. He would often call Mary Belle and pray with her on the phone. At every opportunity, he would visit her. She had become bedridden with congestive heart failure. The family took turns staying with her at her home in Ft. Blackmore, and hospice volunteers visited her as well.

She grew weaker as the weeks passed. Billy was in North Carolina when they called him to come home. They had told him on the phone that she had become unresponsive. She had slipped into a mild coma and had not spoken for twenty-four hours. Billy had made the long trip through the majestic Appalachian Mountains to Ft. Blackmore. As he entered her home, there was a great heaviness in the air. He looked around the living room and noticed objects that brought back memories of his childhood visits with Mary Belle. Familiar sights and smells flooded his mind. He knew this would be the last opportunity to see her, and he hoped she would be able to talk to him.

The family was glad to see Billy. Mary Belle treated Billy more like a son than a grandson. He was her favorite grandchild, and everyone knew it. She used to say, "I love all of my children and grandchildren. I don't make a difference between them; they make the difference in the way they treat me."

Every year, Billy would find time out of his busy schedule to spend a week with Mary Belle. Wherever she wanted to go or whatever she wanted to do, Billy would accommodate her. Their adventures would never be forgotten. Time spent was wisdom earned for Billy. He never tired of her storytelling and laughter. The Great Smoky Mountains was always her favorite place to visit. She loved the Cherokee Reservation in North Carolina. Together they would travel through the mountains and talk for hours on end about everything imaginable. They would take roads less traveled and go to towns tucked away in the foothills of Tennessee, North

Carolina, and Georgia, always stopping for a picnic of home-grown tomato sandwiches along the way. They never tired of each other's company.

Now, here he sat in her living room, staring at the door to her bedroom.

The poignant silence was broken by Bethel's voice. "Go on in. Tell her what you want, but she hasn't talked to anybody since yesterday."

Billy started to the bedroom. He prayed, "Lord, just once more. Let me hear her voice, just once more."

Billy entered the room to see her small, frail body lying in bed. He sat down beside her and stroked her forehead, gliding his fingers along her silver hair. He leaned toward her good ear. She had lost her hearing in the other ear and always cupped one ear when she strained to hear something of importance.

"Granny, this is Billy. I don't know if you can hear me, but I want to thank you. Thank you for being there for me. Thank you for showing me Jesus and for loving me. I love you."

Mary Belle's lips pursed, and she whispered, "I love you, too, honey."

Those were the last words that Billy ever heard her say. God had answered his prayer.

The next few days were foggy. Billy found himself talking with God and reminiscing about his grandmother. He walked the property the next day to look over the land that his grandparents had worked so hard to maintain. He thought about the hikes that he would take on the property when he would come for a visit. He knew these were sacred hills, not only to Mary Belle's family, but to him. He remembered the hours that he spent with God in solitude as he looked out over the hills. He sat down and penned the words to "Sacred Mountains":

> *Let me walk the sacred mountains*
> *In the presence of my God*
> *Let me hear His voice of thunder*
> *While upon these hills I trod*
> *Majestic glory speaks His splendor*
> *Darkest night gives way to dawn*
> *When the morning star arises*
> *Then I'll know that I am home*
> *When the morning star arises*
> *Then I'll know that I am home*

Let me walk the sacred mountains
In the presence of my king
With the holy hosts of heaven
I will lift my heart to sing
Angels shout with hallelujahs
As they circle 'round the throne
Earthly memories are fading
I am now where I belong
Earthly memories are fading
I am now where I belong

Let me walk the sacred mountains
In the presence of my Lord
As I join the saints before me
We will sing in one accord
Rhapsodies of sweet surrender
Overtures of highest praise
Now in heaven, home eternal
I will worship all my days
Now in heaven, home eternal
I will worship all my days

Billy was asked to share something at the funeral in Gate City, Virginia. Billy shared some words and sang a song. The winding trip to the graveside was long and silent. As they stood around the casket for the last time, Billy looked out over the beautiful southwest Virginia mountains. He lifted his voice and sang "Sacred Mountains." Billy knew that he might never return to this place again. A chapter in his life was closed, but the memories of a Godly grandmother would last him a lifetime and have a lasting effect on many souls.

- *Chapter 22* -

Acts of God

The new millennium had come and gone. All of the anxiety of Y2K had settled down. The end of the world had not come to pass, as some had predicted. Billy Wayne's ministry was still growing. Doors were continuing to open for Billy as a singer, songwriter, and speaker, as he was also learning that life brings great blessings and sometimes great loss.

The year 2002 brought bereavement to Billy and his family. Brock, Bethel's husband, passed away on February 16. He had struggled with diabetes for years. He had spent time in and out of the hospital, had been put on peritoneal dialysis, and was slowly going downhill. It was a struggle for Billy to be on the road and not be there for Brock and Bethel. He felt as though he was letting them down. Brock assured Billy, "Don't worry about me. You go and tell as many people about Jesus as you can, so more of them can go to heaven."

Brock eventually ended up in the hospital. The diabetes had taken a toll on his body. Instead of praying for recovery, the family began to commit Brock to Christ's care and pray for mercy. Billy found himself by Brock's side. He watched as Brock's vital signs grew weaker. When Brock took his last breath, Billy saw him at peace for the first time in a long time. Billy finally understood the Scripture, *"Precious in the sight of the Lord is the death of his saints." Psalm 116:15*

Pastor David Salley from Gravelly Baptist Church, who had become a pillar of strength for Billy and his family, helped preach the funeral.

David captured Brock's death that day by sharing a vision about the image of seeing Christ seated at the right hand of God. He spoke of the death of Stephen from the Book of Acts, Chapter 6. Stephen was quoted in verse 56 as saying, "I see heaven open and the Son of Man *standing* at the right hand of God." David said, "When one of God's saints passes, Jesus stands to welcome them." Billy thought about that. When Brock took his last breath in the hospital, Jesus stood and welcomed him home. What comfort Billy found in those words.

Later on that year, Billy would be reminded once again of the price of traveling in full time ministry. He came to find that sacrifices had to be made when following Christ's call. Family and friends would always come second as he yielded himself to absolute surrender. Those around him often tried to make him feel guilty for not being there for them in their time of need. They didn't realize their selfishness would bring incredible guilt. Time and again, Billy would have to weigh what God was calling him to do as opposed to what people expected from him. They never understood how difficult it was for him not to be there when tragedy hit.

After recording *Act of God* with Scotty Wilbanks, the Christian music industry came knocking once more. Leigh Meredith knew that Billy had great potential as a Christian music artist. She knew that he was marketable because of his impact on people all over the country, who always gave him a great reception. She also knew that his album sales were a clear indication of his success. She was burdened to see Billy get the exposure on a national and international label. Leigh had been there both times when the Gospel Music Association had recognized his songwriting abilities. She has seen him perform alongside nationally known music artists and knew that the audiences loved him.

Leigh went to Nashville and met with four of GMA's top independent radio promoters. All four expressed a desire to push Billy in the market. However, Leigh felt drawn to one particular promoter. Barb King was well known in the Christian music scene. She had helped promote Michael W. Smith, New Song, and a slew of other artists. She was well respected by Christian artists and the music industry.

After hearing *Act of God*, Barb knew that God wanted her to help Billy. The only reason she took the time to listen to the album was because of Scotty Wilbanks. Scotty had been a part of New Song, and she wanted to hear what Scotty was up to. After listening to the album, Barb called Leigh and requested some time to visit with her and set up some dates to hear Billy.

Barb traveled to Beaver Dam, Kentucky, to see Billy in concert. She took some time to meet with him and pray. She not only wanted to promote Billy, she wanted to become his manager. She said that she had worked with many artists and felt that God's hand was on Billy and that he needed to have a national platform for people to experience his ministry.

Billy was overwhelmed. He couldn't believe what he was hearing. Barb whisked him off to Nashville for a photo shoot and began to work with her staff on promotional angles. She then came to see him at Mountain Mania in Pigeon Forge. She noticed the devotional handbooks that were being used that week and asked Billy who had written the material. He told her that he had. Barb was stunned. She knew there was more to him than she had originally seen.

After more meetings and prayer, Barb decided that Billy should not only be a Christian music artist, but also strive for a publishing contract for his retreats and devotional guides. She wanted to promote him as a speaker and singer. Barb soon set up showcases for him to perform in Nashville. She had already been contacted by four major labels that were interested in signing him. She preferred a smaller company that hadn't been bought out by a secular label. She was looking for a record label that would also help in publishing his writings.

A showcase was set up for November of 2003. Barb met with Billy's executive board and presented her plans for Billy Wayne Ministries. Everyone was excited and worked hard to meet the demands that had to take place in the near future.

Unfortunately, before the showcase could take place, Barb King received devastating news. Her four-year-old daughter, Olivia, was diagnosed with cystic fibrosis. Everything in her world and at Vision Productions came to a halt. Olivia needed organ transplants. Barb's hopes and dreams for Billy were put on hold.

Even though Billy was disappointed, his main concern was Barb and Olivia. The ministry shifted focus and began to pray for Olivia. Barb had to spend so much time, energy, and money that she could no longer assist Billy. She was very apologetic and rescheduled the showcase for January. She didn't want Billy to do the showcase in November without her being present to represent him. When the new year rolled around, Olivia was still struggling. Barb put her plans to promote Billy on hold indefinitely.

Billy saw this as God's will. Knowing that someone believed in his ministry was the most important thing. Barb's interest showed Billy that he was "good enough" by the world's standards. Even though it was a setback, Billy never lost focus of his calling. This wouldn't keep him from doing what he had been doing for years.

While on his annual mission trip to New York that year, once again bad news came from home. Billy was performing a concert on Hamilton Hill, which is located in Schenectady, near Albany. Billy loved to go to this particular area of Schenectady because the people there were always receptive to God's moving. This section of the city was easily forgotten by most. Drug addicts, prostitutes, and down-and-out people were always attentive to hear about the hope of Christ and his redemptive love. Billy was more than happy to share his Savior with them.

Near the end of the concert, Billy saw his friend, Jim Taylor, standing to the side. Billy knew that Jim and his wife Kelleye had just returned from a visit to Arkansas. Jim shouldn't have been there that night. Billy couldn't figure out what was going on, but he had a feeling that things were not as they should be.

After the concert, Jim asked to speak to Billy.

"Billy, first of all, your brother is alive." Billy's mind raced to think of what could have happened; was one of his brothers in a car accident? Jim continued, "Tonight, your brother, Randy, tried to commit suicide. He's at the hospital now. You need to call home."

Billy was trying to grasp everything that Jim said, yet he wasn't completely shocked by the words. Billy knew that he had traveled this road once before with Randy. There were so many questions that ran through Billy's mind.

Once Billy had called home, he found out what had actually happened. Randy was extremely depressed and had called Bethel. He and his wife, Patti, had been fighting earlier (they seemed to be at odds all the time). Randy had also been drinking and was high on drugs. This had driven him to deeper depression.

While on the phone with Bethel, Randy started talking about shooting himself. They used a cell phone to call 911 to send help to Randy and Patti's residence. Randy pointed the gun at his heart and fired. The bullet jammed in the gun. Randy pointed the gun to his heart and pulled the trigger once more. The gun went off but the bullet missed his heart and hit his lung. Randy thought, *I can't do anything right.* He fired the gun once more. The bullet hit the ceiling as Randy fell onto the bed. The rescue team had reached the house and found Randy lying on a blood-soaked mattress. He was rushed to the hospital, where his family kept vigil over him. One of the people ministering to Randy at the time was Cecil.

Upon hearing this, Billy was numb. Where had he failed Randy? Why hadn't he done more to help his brother? So many questions ...

The next day, Billy was reflecting on all that had happened. He remembered taking the boys in the band to breakfast at Dunkin' Donuts. He thought, *If I can make it to the parking lot, I'll have the guys go inside and I'll be able to let my walls down.*

Billy almost made it. Grief had welled up in him. As soon as they reached the Dunkin' Donuts parking lot, Billy lost it. He began to weep out loud. He couldn't control his emotions any more. The thought of losing his younger brother overwhelmed him. Shane, the drummer and road manager, put his arm around Billy to comfort him. The other guys followed suit. They prayed for Billy. Billy had always prayed for them. Now, they were giving back.

After the trip to New York was over, Billy went back to visit his family in Tennessee. Randy was very receptive to Billy's words and comfort as Billy challenged him to listen to God. Billy wished so much that he could just hand over the peace and comfort of the Holy Spirit to his brother, but he knew Randy first had to accept it. He told Randy that God had a great purpose for his life and that God wasn't finished with him yet.

Randy grew stronger over the next few months. Spring rolled around and Billy was producing and directing the Easter production in Eden. Randy found himself visiting to see the production. The whole cast and crew had been praying for Randy for years, and now here he was. At the end of the show, when Pastor Steve Griffith invited the audience to come forward, Randy stepped up and committed his life to Christ.

Even though this was a great step for Randy, his addictions would continue to haunt him and try to rob him. Satan had claimed territory in Randy's life that he wasn't going to let go of easily. The talons of depression had planted themselves deep into his mind, and Randy would battle the scars from his suicide attempt for a great many years to follow.

More changes were on the rise in Billy Wayne's ministry. In 2003, the rent on Broad Street had risen to $1,000 a month. Billy felt a need to invest in real estate rather than waste the money on rent.

After much searching and prayer, God presented a piece of property, the old Beechwood Family Entertainment Center in Fall Branch, Tennessee, right outside Kingsport. Billy was in Eden at the time. Leigh felt that the fourteen-acre property had great potential and had sent Billy a videotape of the complex, which consisted of a 4,000-square-foot home, a 2,400-square-foot garage/storage building, and a 10,000-square-foot theatre.

At the same time this property became available, the Lee Greenwood Theatre in Pigeon Forge was for sale. Some pastors and businessmen from Sevierville, Tennessee, contacted Billy to see if he would be interested in moving his ministry to Pigeon Forge. This would mean that the theatre would be owned by someone else, but Vision Productions would act as a management company and producers of the shows. Billy had seen what happened when owners and producers aren't in agreement. Kingdom Resort was a great example of business before ministry. If he decided to do this, he would be taking a risk. He was not sure about having someone else in charge; he would be subject to their vision and direction.

Billy was tempted once again to follow his own desires. To move his ministry into the Lee Greenwood Theatre, with its great facilities, would be a once-in-a-lifetime opportunity. He would have to seek the will of God in this decision, but he already knew that God would say no.

Billy found himself lying on the stage at Beechwood, on his face, before God. He looked around the building. The building had seen better days. It had so much potential, but it was a far cry from a finished theatre.

> *What do you want, Lord? This building needs so much work. It would be so much easier to move to Pigeon Forge. I want what you want, but look at this place. It looks like a barn.*
>
> God's response was simple and profound: *"Jesus started in a stable. Just trust me."*

After a great deal of prayer, the ministry purchased the property for $175,000 and Vision Productions, Inc., Billy Wayne Ministries moved to Fall Branch. The mortgage payment for the property was about $1,150 a month. This was only $150 more than the rent on Broad Street. The upstairs of the house was turned into office space. The basement of the house became a retreat area for mission teams and ministers. It also housed the maintenance staff. The upstairs of the garage/storage building was converted to the wardrobe department. The downstairs was made into prop storage and a workshop for set construction.

The ministry had no funds for renovations, so other than the sounds of demolition, the theatre stood silent for over a year. Finally, in the fall of 2004, someone stepped forward to finance $185,000 for renovations and construction. Mission teams came from all over the eastern United States to help with the project. In the spring of 2005, LampLight Theatre opened with the performance of Billy's original Easter production, *More than Just a Man*.

With the relocation of the ministry, God began to shift his servants once more. Leigh Meredith, Billy's partner, was called to work at Celebration Church as the singles ministry coordinator. This was one of the most difficult transitions that Billy and Leigh would experience. While still having a desire to serve the ministry, she knew God was calling her outside her comfort zone.

As God willed, Leigh left Vision Productions after nine years of service. God had already begun to work in the hearts of others to come and take positions in the ministry to help fulfill the new vision of LampLight Theatre. Larry and Mary McClure felt led of God to sell all they had and move to Kingsport to help Billy. Both had been involved in the dramas at Osborne Baptist Church in Eden.

Mary would soon head up the wardrobe department as head costumer. Larry would become theatre manager and helped in all aspects of running LampLight Theatre. They were a great team and made certain the productions were all that Billy envisioned.

It was at this time in Billy's life that God threw him a curve ball. Just as Billy was content in his "singlehood," along came Kimberly Holbrook. Billy had met Kimberly at a singles event hosted by Leigh Meredith at Celebration Church. Billy was slated to speak at this particular event. Kim, who was divorced, was there with her boyfriend at the time, Dennis Carmen.

After hearing Billy that night, Kim and her friend, Susan Depew, decided to go to a singles retreat that Vision Productions was hosting in Fries, Virginia. They had encouraged Dennis and Susan's cousin, John, to attend with them.

As Billy spoke that weekend, God began to convict Kim's heart. She knew that after her divorce, she had not been where she needed to be. She allowed her "busyness" to get in the way of her relationship with Jesus. God used the retreat to refocus her life. It was this reawakening of her walk with Christ that drew her to Billy Wayne Ministries. She began to see the need for more exposure to the ministry.

Kim had worked for fourteen years at Eastman Chemical Corporation as a trade show manager. She had traveled all over the country and around the world as a spokesperson for the company. She was great at her job and was highly respected. She had worked very hard to achieve her position at the corporation. Little did she know that God was going to use those gifts to glorify Him.

After a series of meetings with Billy, Kim knew what she had to do. Through the prompting of the Holy Spirit, Kim broke off her relationship with Dennis. She felt that she needed to spend more time with God as He was calling her to ministry. As hard as she fought, God's prompting was stronger. Kim finally yielded to the Lord and left Eastman to go to work as artist relations manager for Vision Productions.

Billy and Kim developed a close relationship as Billy started feeling drawn to her. He wanted her to know everything that was going on in his life. He couldn't wait to see her or talk to her. He felt like a school boy.

> *What is wrong with me? This is crazy. I can't be falling in love. I'm in my forties. I've accepted the fact that I will be single the rest of my life. Why now, God?*

No matter how many questions Billy had, the fact remained that he was falling in love with Kim. It wasn't long after this that Billy and Kim began to date. With every bit of understanding that this could be his future wife, Billy allowed his heart to be opened. Perhaps this relationship was meant to be, for reasons beyond Billy's understanding. For years, Billy thought he had been called to be single. Now, the possibility of marriage was staring him in the face.

As time progressed, people placed a great deal of pressure on Billy and Kim to get engaged and marry. Things seemed to be moving too fast. People wanted to see a ring and a commitment on Billy's part. The pressure was too much. Billy found himself pulling away from Kim. He felt that he could never be all that Kim wanted or needed. After much soul searching and agonizing, Billy broke off the relationship with her.

Looking back, Billy realized some important truths. He had doubted that anyone could ever love him. He wondered if he could ever love again. This relationship answered both those doubts. Kim showed great patience with this whole process. She gave Billy the space he needed to figure out what God wanted. As a result, their friendship stayed intact as they continued to work together. The whole time, their relationship was based around Jesus. They always kept Christ in the center of everything. God had used Kim to restore worth to Billy that he somehow lost in the process of pursuing God's will.

God continued to use both of them as a team to reach many for Christ. He brought two people together that needed to understand the male/

female dynamic the way that God intended. Billy would always feel guilty about the break-up. He knew that he was afraid of dividing his devotion between God and Kim. He knew that this relationship, as any, would require time and attention. He wasn't certain if he was willing to do that. Christ had been his first love for so long. He wasn't sure that he wanted to give that up, and he was satisfied with that. Billy knew it was his choice concerning Kim. He also knew that there was a great deal of peace that came in letting go of the relationship. It was an adjustment that both of them would have to make.

Despite Billy's decision to end their romantic involvement, Kim remained faithful to her call to Vision Productions; she continued to support Billy as her friend. She knew that God wasn't finished with her and that there was ministry that had yet to be done.

- *Chapter 23* -

God Is Still Watching

Billy spent much of the day on March 7, 2007, reflecting over the last twenty years of his life. He was turning forty-four years old on that day. Though he knew, beyond a shadow of a doubt, that he had gone down the path God had given him, he couldn't help but wonder what life would have been like if he had married and had children of his own. He calculated that his own children would probably be teenagers by now. Entertaining the thought only briefly, he quickly turned his mind to other things. Billy doubted that he would ever have children of his own. Becoming a father was a far-fetched fantasy, since he had never married, a silent dream he too often found himself nurturing. He had played many roles in all the productions he had been involved with in his life. He often rehearsed the role of a father, never thinking it would become a reality. Billy silently watched the parenting skills of the people in his life and wondered if he would be as good as them.

In late March 2007, a young man walked inside LampLight Theatre to do community service. Ridgemond Anthony "Ridge" Mosley was a sixteen-year-old, high-risk student with a shaded past. His social worker, Cindy Shelton, knew that Billy Wayne would be the perfect influence for Ridge. She knew that all he needed was a relationship with Jesus Christ.

Billy and the staff took Ridge under their wing and began to nurture him with the love of Jesus. Ridge attended Vision Productions' Senior I'm Accepted (I.A.) Camp (for underprivileged students) in June. He came to Billy after the second day and told Billy that he wasn't like the rest of the students there; he confided to Billy that the other students had something he didn't. Finding that paternal character he longed to play, Billy shared the truth of the simple gospel to Ridge. That day Ridge gave his life to Christ and began a journey that would take him places he had never dreamed.

Ridge finally trusted Billy enough to share the pain of his family with him. He had grown up in a single parent home with a mother who had a drug addiction. Ridge's mother had him declared mentally challenged as a child. This entitled her to a monthly check from the government. It wasn't until his eighth grade year that Ridge realized that he was not mentally challenged. Ridge learned how to endure going from place to place as his mother sought out love and acceptance from different men.

Ridge, like Billy, was a survivor and was determined to rise above his situation. He ended up hanging out with Vision Productions interns during the summer of 2007 and became great friends with Billy's younger cousin, Preston Vermillion. Ridge was experiencing a freedom and acceptance that he had never had before.

August 2007 brought tragedy. As with any new Christian, all Hell on earth broke loose on Ridge. Ridge's mother had a live-in boyfriend with whom she shared two sons. Because of Ridge's newfound relationship with Christ, his home became a house of turmoil. His mother's boyfriend threw Ridge out of the home. Preston loaded up Ridge's few belongings and brought him to LampLight Theatre.

Preston called Billy and told him about the situation. In turn, Billy called Cindy Shelton for advice. Cindy asked Billy if he would be willing to take custody of Ridge. Billy panicked, realizing the inadequacies and selfishness that singlehood had afforded him. He told Cindy that he would pray about it.

Once again, God had already laid the foundation for the events that would follow. Over the next few weeks, Billy and Ridge would find themselves before lawyers, judges, and social workers. Courtrooms became very familiar to them. In September 2007, Billy and Cindy convinced Ridge's mother to sign full legal guardianship of Ridge over to Billy Wayne. After she did so, Ridge moved in with Billy. He often looked at Ridge with awe, realizing how God had orchestrated both of their lives for such a time as this.

Billy learned from first-hand experience what it was to be a father figure, to have someone looking to only you to meet their needs and answer their questions. Ridge's birth certificate lists no name for his father, but for the first time, Ridge had the father he thought he would never have.

In August 2008, as Billy rode from Tennessee to New York, he sat contentedly, looking out the window and preparing himself for the mission trip that lay ahead. He knew he would encounter hopelessness in the hearts of many New Yorkers in the form of drug addiction, homelessness, depression, and the occult. These were all demons he had seen before, robbing their victims of joy and life. He prayed that God would prepare his heart and soul to help the people he would come in contact with over the next couple of weeks.

As he prayed he began to ponder his own personal journey through life, realizing he could just as easily have been one of those people struggling with drug addiction or depression. Why had God seen fit to raise him from the ashes of his youth to hold such a high calling? How could this poor boy from the foothills of the Appalachian Mountains become an ambassador for the King?

It was in that moment that God gave him a greater understanding of where he had been as well as where he was going.

> *Billy, you were born with a strong will. I put that in you. I knew what the finished product of "you" would be. I was there in every moment of your life. When you almost died as an infant, I was there for your mama. I gave her hope and held her as she wept for you. She asked Me to take her life instead of yours. You see, I was pursuing Bethel as well as keeping you alive. She had invited Me into her life before you were ever born, but she had forgotten.*
>
> *I turned my face away when your daddy called you names, for I knew the pain it caused you. It pained me as well, for I love Cecil as much as I love you. He loved you then too, Billy, but he had walked in disobedience to My Word and had become indifferent. He was actually angry at Me and himself, not you.*
>
> *The training ground you walked daily as a young man would someday be the reason for your strength and perseverance. The ministry I have called you to has not been an easy road, but a weaker man without proper training would have given up by now.*
>
> *All the nights you cried yourself to sleep, I was standing guard over you. I fought off the demons of depression and worthlessness continually. Everything about your young life was a breeding ground for them, so I protected you all the more. I kept them from getting a stronghold on*

you. Every prayer you whispered in your childlike faith I breathed in like sweet perfume.

Like an Olympic athlete training to win the gold medal, your past along with everything you've ever gone through has been the arena for your training to become an ambassador for My Kingdom.

Stay strong in My teaching. Don't go astray. Love as I love. Remain confident in the face of adversity and remember ...

I am with you always.

Billy came to the realization that this is what he was made for. Through his weaknesses and struggles, God would do something that only He could do. Billy would find himself many times asking God to do for him what he could not do for himself.

Being credited as a man of great faith, Billy Wayne has often lightheartedly commented, "I'm not sure I have such great faith. I think God just feels sorry for me. I think God looks at me and says, 'Bless his heart. He really believes that I am going to come through for him.' I'm not sure if that is childlike faith or stupidity. Either way, I am blessed. God keeps answering my prayers."

One might ask, "Why does Billy continue to do all the things he does?"

His answer would be simple and straightforward: "I have no choice. At some point I'm not making the choices anymore. I am simply yielding to the call of God at every turn. God keeps using me and those who minister alongside me because we keep saying 'Yes.'"

Billy knows he will rest when he gets to heaven. Until then he will be a servant of God who is out there sharing with those broken souls who have time to listen. As servant who can see the pain in hurting hearts, he will surrender his own will to be able to point others to the hope that set him free.

Billy will always be looking for that one life that needs Christ most. He will listen to God's voice as he stands to deliver the message of Jesus. He will always be more interested in pleasing God than pleasing man. It will continue to cost him everything.

Fame may never come his way. Fortune will never cloud his vision. Billy Wayne is a man on a mission from God. He will never rest until he sees his Savior face to face.

He is a man who would never change a thing from his past and knows God placed him right where He wanted him. Billy will never use his parents or his struggles as excuses for not being everything God has called him to be. He will never deny his weaknesses but will give God the glory for his strength. He knows that he is nothing without Jesus. Having Jesus guiding him, he knows there is no limit to what God can do in his life, which has been yielded to the Spirit.

Billy will spend the rest of his life on others. Everything he has gone through points others to a Savior that came to redeem us all.

On a stormy night in the mountains of southwestern Virginia, God watched as a little child was born in the midst of chaos. It was with a great purpose and plan that God watched over this child's life as he grew. Billy Wayne accepted the calling God placed on his life.

And God is still watching.

Epilogue

Billy entered the realm of Christian music in the fall of 1981. His leap into full-time music evangelism began in January of 1989. Since that time, he has been privileged to work with many recording artists and world-renowned producers, including Dan Mukala and Scotty Wilbanks (New Song and Third Day). He has had several opportunities to sign with a major record label, including with Grant Cunningham of EMI Records. Unfortunately, Grant went home to be with the Lord before all the details were worked out. Billy felt that God's timing was perfect, and at the time of each opportunity, God was saying "no." Billy's desire was to never compromise his ministry or his integrity in a trade-off for the opportunity to be a part of the Christian music industry.

Billy made it his prayer always to be able to offer the ministry free of charge. He has never set a fee nor charged to preach or minister at a church. He struggled with the concept of charging admission for the performances at LampLight Theatre. Knowing the theatre could not continue to offer the level of excellence and professionalism needed, the decision was made to put in place a suggested donation for the performances.

In the mid-1990s, Billy started I'm Accepted (I.A.) Camps for underprivileged children and high-risk students. He attended a weeklong Wilds Christian Camp once as a child and had worked hard to raise enough money to get to go. He sold Krispy Kreme donuts, washed cars, and saved money from his newspaper route, which earned him enough funds to get a good start on the cost of the camp. Carolyn and Raymond

Hammond at Tabernacle Baptist Church paid the rest of his scholarship. This camp changed his life.

He never forgot that camp experience and prayed that the Lord would let him offer camp to students who would not otherwise be able to attend. Thousands of students later and countless lives changed, God has been faithful in making that dream come true through the generous donations from churches and individuals.

The ministry continues to host retreats for singles and married couples. Even though Billy has never been married, some of his most popular retreats are for married couples. He knows that the principles of a good marriage are based on a person's personal relationship with Christ. If that is in order, then the rest will fall into place.

Each year, Vision Productions sponsors two mission trips: one to Brownsville, Texas/Matamoros, Mexico, and the other to upstate New York and New York City.

In crossing paths with people like Shawn Bennett, Billy developed a burden to work with people in crisis situations. He began a mentorship program that provides the opportunity for Vision Productions to work with individuals that are struggling with chemical addictions, family problems, or spiritual crises. This program works with individuals to give them a stable environment and prepares them to go forward with their life through accountability once they leave.

Vision Productions also works with students and adults who get into legal trouble and have to perform community service. This partnership allows Billy to speak to these individuals and to encourage them in their spiritual walk. This gives the ministry opportunities to inspire these people to make the right choices.

The ministry also offers internships to college-age students that want to get experience in working in a ministry setting. Throughout the year, the ministry takes on individuals and trains them in different aspects of ministry whether it be in the office, theatre, or on the road in music evangelism.

Since 1995, Billy has been traveling with an accompanist or a band. This has allowed him a great deal of freedom. Music accompaniment tracks held Billy back sometimes, especially during worship. Having people on the road with him also led the ministry to a higher level of accountability. Billy has always seen this as an opportunity to mentor young musicians while using their talents for ministry. Some of these young musicians have had a lasting impression on Billy's life and ministry.

Todd Westfall was Billy's first road manager. Todd had been involved with the same singles ministry as Leigh Meredith. They both came to work for Billy's ministry at the same time. During his stay at Vision Productions, Todd was called to full-time youth ministry. Todd moved to Hurricane, West Virginia, and accepted a position as a youth minister.

Keith Glover became a dear friend of Billy's through Keith's sister Connie McMullins, who worked for the ministry. Keith became Billy's road manager and worked with Billy's ministry on several occasions. While working at Vision Productions, Keith was also called to full-time youth ministry. He was ordained at Osborne Baptist Church and became the youth minister there. He and his wife Melissa soon moved back to East Tennessee, where he held positions as youth minister and associate pastor. He is credited with establishing home churches and is currently serving as a pastor in the Johnson City, Tennessee, area.

Billy worked with Jonathan and Joel Caldwell for several years. Billy met them through the same singles ministry where Leigh Meredith served. Both came from traveling evangelism led by their father. Billy, Jonathan, and Joel sang together for several years. They led retreats, camps, and youth functions throughout West Virginia, Indiana, and South Carolina. Both went on to be youth pastors in West Virginia and currently travel with the Power Team Ministry throughout the United States. Jonathan and his wife, Greta, currently reside in Texas, where Jonathan is involved on the corporate level of the Power Team Ministry.

Kyle Dillard worked as a guitarist and soloist for Vision Productions. He and his wife, Teresa Stilgenbauer, moved to the Chicago area, where Kyle became the junior high praise and worship leader for Willow Creek Community Church. They later moved to the Charlotte area, where he is serving as the music minister at the Cove.

Chad Darst, from Point Pleasant, West Virginia, served as a guitarist and vocalist with Billy. He married Betsy Gauldin, from Eden, North Carolina, and has served on the praise and worship team at Osborne Baptist Church. Chad is also a music producer and helps young Christian artists develop their skills.

Wendy Rollins was also from Point Pleasant, West Virginia. She is the only female that traveled as a band member with Billy. She played the piano and sang duets and back-up with Billy. She brought soul and incredible vocal talent to the ministry. Wendy left the ministry and soon afterward was diagnosed with a brain tumor. Wendy went home to be with the Lord in 2007. She served Jesus Christ well and will be cherished forever.

Trey Dishner, a very talented worship leader from the Tri-Cities area, lent his vocal gifts and piano/keyboard skills to Billy's band in 2003. When Trey, Wendy, and Chad were with the band, they coined the name "Wayniacs."

Billy saw Shane Ayers grow up at Osborne Baptist Church in Eden, North Carolina. Having an eye for talent and seeing that Shane had the heart of a servant, Billy asked him to play drums in his first band. Shane served as a drummer for Billy for three years. He became a backbone for Billy's musical productions. Shane also acted as road manager for Billy and became a close friend and confidant. Shane left Billy's ministry to marry Amy Wise, from Waynesburg, Pennsylvania. Shane attended mortuary school and is a funeral director at Milliken and Throckmorton Funeral Home in Waynesburg, under Daryl Throckmorton (a Vision Productions executive board member). Shane is currently playing for a praise team at the Church of the Nazarene and is now a father.

Billy met Brian Jackson at a concert in Bishopville, South Carolina. Billy felt led to ask Brian to join him without even hearing him play. Two weeks later, Brian joined the ministry. Brian traveled with Billy for a couple of years accompanying him on guitar. Billy helped Brian develop as a solo artist and praise and worship leader. After being led to move, Brian became a praise and worship leader at a new church in Camden, South Carolina. He moved to Hilton Head and married his sweetheart, Holly. He continues his music today.

In following the leading of the Holy Spirit, Billy knew there was a great need to have a band. He prayed for God to send him talented musicians with a heart for ministry. While performing a concert in Riner, Virginia, in 2000, Billy met some young musicians that opened for him. Josh Reedy and Brian Bunn became an answer to Billy's prayer. Josh and Brian traveled with Billy on and off for about four years as Seven Day Rest and Soul Divine. Josh brought inspiration to Billy and his music. Billy could always rely on Josh to help in writing new worship songs and bringing his music to life. Josh contributed a great deal to making Billy's ministry go forward.

Throughout their time with Billy, Josh and Brian were challenged and mentored to be men of God. They learned what music evangelism was about while giving their best as musicians. Billy gave their band many opportunities to open for him and share their music with his audiences. Knowing it was time for them to go on to greater things, Billy hooked them up with Scotty Wilbanks, who in turn facilitated an agreement with a major label. Josh and Brian (together with Eric Miker, see below) formed the group DecembeRadio and signed with Spring Hill (Slanted) Records. DecembeRadio was nominated in 2007 for a Grammy and four Dove Awards. Billy was present at the Dove Awards when they were voted Christian Rock Artists of the Year and also in 2009, when they received two more Dove Awards.

Billy continues to have a great relationship with them and partners with them on occasion to do ministry. He still offers advice and encouragement in their lives and ministry. In the fall of 2008, Billy served as road pastor for their "Satisfied" tour.

In 2006, Billy had the opportunity to officiate the marriage between Josh Reedy and Rachel Throckmorton, daughter of Vision Production's board member, Daryl Throckmorton, from Waynesburg. They now reside in Christiansburg, Virginia.

Eric Miker became a great friend to Billy. Billy had encouraged Eric's youth group in Shinnston, West Virginia, to start a praise team, so they did, calling themselves *Twist of Faith*, and Eric showed great promise. Billy asked Eric to travel and play for him, overcoming a great many obstacles along the way. Billy encouraged Eric to listen to God's call over everyone's opinion. Eric grew exceptionally in his walk of faith. He traveled with Billy for over a year and then joined Josh and Brian in DecembeRadio.

Billy participated in Eric's wedding to his wife, Donielle, in 2007.

Nick Ours was Billy's music director and accompanist in 2004 and 2005. Nick was a guitar teacher for Los Angeles Music Institute for several years before coming to Vision Productions. Billy met Nick in Shinnston, West Virginia, on one of his many visits to Shinnston First Baptist's youth outreach facility, the Lighthouse. Nick moved back to Shinnston to continue leading worship and mentoring other young musicians in the area.

Jared Bryant served as interim accompanist for Billy's ministry in 2005. Billy had the opportunity to see Jared grow as a singer in Twist of Faith; he developed into a talented guitarist and worship leader. Jared and his wife, Jill, have become great supporters of Billy. Jared is currently working in the social services field in Parkersburg, West Virginia, and serves on the worship team and with the youth ministry at North Parkersburg Baptist Church.

Dave Wray has served on many occasions as a bass player with different bands that have accompanied Billy. Dave is a cancer survivor and a walking example of God's healing power. He still plays with Billy when the opportunity arises and brings a whole new meaning to Billy's song, "Soul Survivor." Billy considers Dave a hero. Dave and his wife Lindsey were married in 2009, and he is currently in graduate school in West Virginia.

Alan Mustian and Adam Minter served as summer musician interns in 2006. Both Alan and Adam attended Liberty University. Adam served as Billy's drummer and began playing the guitar and writing songs while with Billy. Adam finished his first solo album in 2007, with Chad Darst as his producer. Alan is a talented guitarist and songwriter who graduated from Liberty in 2010 and is currently serving as worship leader in Henderson, North Carolina. Billy had the privilege to officiate the wedding of Alan Mustian and his wife, Erica, in March 2010.

Billy has had the opportunity to work with and act as spiritual mentor to an exceptionally talented band named 7 Miles. Benton Blount, Wes Brown (the band's founding member), and Brandon Beal have become dear friends and colleagues of Billy. While busy schedules often keep them apart, they occasionally work together on recording projects and live shows. They have been wonderful partners in ministry. Doors in the Christian music industry continue to open for 7 Miles. They reside in Nashville and continue their career in music ministry.

Jason Wilson served with Billy for over two years and was an incredible asset. Jason is from Bishopville, South Carolina, and is a talented singer/songwriter and guitarist. Billy had the opportunity to perform the wedding ceremony between Jason and Jennifer Slaughter in May 2008. Jason and Jennifer moved to Eden, North Carolina, in August of 2008, where Jason serves as youth minister at Osborne Baptist Church.

Throughout the years, God used these and other gifted musicians and friends to challenge Billy in music and ministry. Countless interns have been mentored through Billy's ministry and continue to pursue their calling to spread the gospel of Jesus Christ.

Over the years, God has given Billy numerous songs, many of which have debuted on his eighteen-plus recording projects from 1989 to 2010. In 2000, "The Call" slotted Billy as a regional finalist in Washington DC for Spotlight Song of the Year with the Gospel Music Association.

Billy has performed over 5,600 evangelistic concerts throughout the United States and Mexico. Thousands of people have trusted Christ as their personal Lord and Savior. Countless others have grown in their walk of faith.

Under Billy Wayne's direction, LampLight Theatre has seen over 6,000 people make a profession of faith for salvation in a five-year period because of the message presented in the productions.

As of spring 2011, Vision Productions, Inc., Billy Wayne Ministries staff consists of the following:

ADMINISTRATIVE STAFF

Executive Administrator	Neawonna Arrants (Billy's cousin)
Financial Administrator	Carolyn Woods
Events Coordinator/Office Assistant	Andrea Begley (Billy's stepsister)

LAMPLIGHT THEATRE STAFF

Theatre Manager/Box Office	Terry Jones
Maintenance Supervisor	Tyler McMullins
Grounds	Cecil Arrington (Billy's father)
Gift Shop	Lois Arrington (Billy's stepmother)

MINISTRY TEAM

Road Manager/Ministry Assistant	Jacob Phillips Band/ "Tattered Saints"
	Jacob Phillips, Carmen Phillips, Tyler McMullins,
	Derek Cress
Booking/Merchandising	Carmen Phillips
Artistic Director	Mary McClure
Road Assistant	Ridge Mosley (Billy's son)

EXECUTIVE BOARD OF DIRECTORS

Chairman	Daryl Throckmorton
Vice-Chairman	Rev. Randall Spivey
Ministerial Vice-Chairman	Rev. Steve Pate
Secretary	Peg Spurlin
Treasurer	Kathy Greeson
Outreach/Prayer	Nancy Vannoy
Advisor	Rev. Dan Tilley